Pam,

Best of luck in
Training your
enterprise with
online marketing

[signature]

MARKETING MIRACLES

Published by CelebrityPress™, Orlando, FL
A division of The Celebrity Branding Agency®

Celebrity Branding® is a registered trademark
Printed in the United States of America.

ISBN: 9780985714314
LCCN: 2012941308

Most CelebrityPress™ titles are available at special quantity discounts for bulk purchases for sales promotions, premiums, fundraising, and educational use. Special versions or book excerpts can also be created to fit specific needs.

For more information, please write:

CelebrityPress™,
520 N. Orlando Ave, #2,
Winter Park, FL 32789

or call 1.877.261.4930

Visit us online at www.CelebrityPressPublishing.com

MARKETING MIRACLES

Odd, Unusual, BREAKTHROUGH STRATEGIES that build great businesses!

TABLE OF CONTENTS

CHAPTER 1

HOW DO MARKETING 'MIRACLES' REALLY OCCUR?

BY DAN S. KENNEDY

L et's start with my disagreements with some of the contributing authors in this book. We have differences. But, if we were in complete agreement all but one of us would be unnecessary. Marketing is not religion. There is no *one* right book, nor even a good argument between warring factions over which is *the* right book. Marketing is situational and fungible and flexible, its treasured absolutes often successfully violated. What makes it interesting enough to be a life of work as it has been for me, and what lets it produce so many amazing opportunities, is that there is more than one way to be right, especially by application, but even by principle. This is why those of us who create wealth for ourselves and others through marketing test, test, test and test some more and even test things we personally wager against and believe will fail. When Einstein was asked how he came to his discoveries, he replied: "I grope." That is exactly how we get to what is called "a control" in print, direct-mail, broadcast or on the web: we grope. We test a matrix of possibilities in theme, copy appeals, offer, formats, etc., etc. and etc. until we get to something that works sufficiently well to continue its use, then we usually keep testing one variable at a time against the control. We do as much initial and on-going testing as the size and scope of the opportunity will allow. This is not good news for the person looking for just ten commandments (or fewer). Or for the means of miracles.

Which brings me to my second preface remark: I'm not in love with the 'Miracles' in this book's title. When you see an advertiser or marketer walking on water, he has placed stones beneath the surface. When you see one of us successfully defy the laws of economic gravity, there is a rope you can't see. Creating an advertising or marketing success of epic proportions or an on-going foundation of strong marketing supporting a small business, professional practice or sales career does involve *some* creativity, but is mostly diligent, often mundane hard work. There's nothing miraculous about it. As Edison described invention: 1% inspiration, 99% perspiration.

If "groping" and "hard work" weren't what you had in mind, it's very likely a "marketing miracle" will stay beyond your grasp, your entire life. I have many clients who have been with me for 10, 20, even 30 years, and, through marketing, have metamorphosed from poor to rich, from unknown to famous, even from ignominious repute to respect and prestige; who have built businesses from zero to $1-billion, from 4 local clinics to a 360 clinic national chain, or who have more quietly created high 6-figure to multi-7-figure incomes in a variety of "ordinary" businesses. They groped, together we groped. They worked like few work. On their projects, I worked like few will work. They and we still grope. They and we still work. "Putting it on auto-pilot" is a fool's fantasy.

In this chapter written exclusively for this book, I will give you a few "micro directions" to categories of market-driven and marketing-driven opportunity, and refer you to additional information about whichever intrigue you. But I want to first and foremost more broadly tell you the truth behind all great marketing successes – regardless of what you might observe from the outside. I have just explained two truths. The third is more specific: multi-media, multi-step integration. Bluntly, anybody who advises focus on one media to the neglect or exclusion of others is either selling that media or ignorant, naïve or stupid, or both, and to you, they are dangerous. Beware. The worst number in business is One. One *anything*. And just for the record, the internet offers a collection of online media. *Media*. Confusing a web site with a business is common insanity. Insanity is harmful enough, but engaging in *common* insanity is especially harmful. You won't find a sustained, sustainable business living on any one media, or these days, living entirely offline or living entirely online. Not one. Even Google must use direct-mail to sell its online advertising services to business, and is steadily increasing its investment in snail-mail year to year. J. Crew Co. mails 40-million paper 'n ink catalogs a year. My client Guthy-Renker's flagship brand, Proactiv, an acne treatment, generates over $800-million a year not thanks to the TV infomercials that fueled it as infant, but thanks to a mix of TV, radio, magazine, local newspaper FSI's (free standing inserts), even Yellow Pages ads, and more media, and thanks to an offline-online integration strategy supporting it in maturity.

One last caution. There is a delusional tendency to think that much is new. A worse tendency is to ignore history in toto as well as history of the industry or profession one is in, thinking it of no useful current purpose; at best a curiosity – certainly *not* a valid source of business plans, strategy, format. The term for this is: willful ignorance. Were I having to hire (thank the stars, I'm not) people to fill skill positions, say copywriter or salesperson, etc., I would give them a relevant *history* test, and pass on the ignorant.

Someone young with an absent background and historical knowledge thinks he is seeing many things for the first time when, in actuality, they are re-treads of things done many times before by many predecessors, and in many instances, done better. He then copycats the already well diluted, many times copied copy, creating derivative weakness when he might have traced to earlier and earlier sources and from those built a much more powerful and profitable asset of his own.

If, for example, you have studied contemporary copywriters but ignored Bernays or Collier, you are at disadvantage.

Nearly all my successes in authorship, speaking, speaking to sell, publishing and business have been brought about by circumventing the contemporary and reaching back, often way back, to draw on the past. A lot of people are fooled by the existence of new technology, from it getting the idea there are new rules, that somehow the reasons why money moves about in the marketplace are also altered and new. In America, we are imperiled as a society by at least two generations taught so little truthful history and so disinterested in it, that they cannot even recognize the thoroughly discredited premises of socialism being aggressively advanced. They remind me of the woman in the TV commercial, with very poor eyesight, coaching a raccoon in through her sliding glass door, to join her in bed – thinking it's "Momma's cat." Similarly, many think my cautions about online and social media that of a fuddy-duddy, but if asked to describe the rise and fall of other media once heralded as panacean or as replacement, they are ignorant. Some are even ignorant of MySpace – *that*, to them, is ancient, irrelevant history. Many think my constant caution against over-dependence on any one media is blathering, but they forget, discount or, often, are ignorant of the sudden disappearance by government decree of, in regressive order, voice broadcast marketing, "cold" tele-marketing, broadcast fax, certain direct-mail formats, TV infomercials – the latter outlawed for many years until Reagan's de-regulation.

Part of the work required for great marketing and of rich marketers is thorough study of, even fascination with the history of their industry, the history of advertising, marketing and direct marketing, and historical framework for understanding human psychology and behavior as well as the movement of money. In advertising, we used to say that giving a typewriter to a monkey did not make him a copywriter. The same can be said about more modern technology and media.

With all that said as preliminary remarks, I'll deliver something you may find more to your liking: specific GPS instructions, pointing to marketing applications that frequently produce giant breakthroughs in varied businesses:

PLACE STRATEGY

Many seeming "marketing miracles" occur by moving a product, service or business from its traditional, customary or common place(s) to another place – and by place I don't necessarily mean geography; I mean media or distribution channel. Proactiv: movement from the drugstore shelf first to the TV infomercial, then to virtually all direct-response media. Amazon and Zappos (acquired by Amazon) began by moving books and shoes from physical stores where people browse and shop to web stores, where people conveniently buy. The marketer behind the now iconic Charles Atlas exercise products took its ads to the pages of comic books.

Often, there is movement from the B2B place to the consumer place or vice versa. My friend, the late Joe Cossman made one of his many million dollar fortunes moving a product originally conceived as a teaching tool to be sold to schools for their biology and earth-science classrooms to the toy store shelf for consumers: The Ant Farm. A client of mine took an industrial chemical that dissolves adhesives to QVC, as a household "miracle" product that gets gum out of kids' hair, easily removes sticky labels from gifts and has 101 other uses. In reverse, both the microwave and the computer were invented for commercial use – and everyone involved with both at their births and infancy could not imagine anybody having them in their homes for personal use. The pricey "massage recliners" now sold in all sorts of catalogs, at Brookstone stores in malls, and at other retailers contain a rolling massage device built for and used in professional massage tables for chiropractic offices.

One of the most interesting Place Strategies is out of category advertising. My clients at Gardner's Mattress, a very high-end mattress store in Lancaster, Pennsylvania, do very well advertising in the Yellow Pages – in the Chiropractic category. Guthy-Renker places ads for Proactiv in the Dermatologist category in Yellow Pages nationwide. I suppose it's "cheating", but it's definitely effective. I own racehorses, and at every horse auction I attend, a jewelry store has set up shop – *if he can have another $10,000 horse, I can have a $10,000 diamond bracelet.*

PROCESS STRATEGY

From one to one to one to many selling has changed countless businesses and made countless fortunes. I have a client who books between $250,000.00 and $1-million of dentistry in a single 2 hour time block via his in-office Implant Seminars. Do you have any idea how many one to one appointments you'd have to run, each at least an hour in length, on average getting one out of three, four or five potential patients to accept treatment, in order to book $1-million in dentistry?

I have developed a very sophisticated process for deliberately delaying a sale, and delivering what I have termed a "shock 'n awe package" before a prospective client or patient is met with, to create profound preference, pre-determination and price elasticity – and we have very successfully implemented this strategy in financial services, health care, weight-loss, home remodeling and other fields. (A small caution: many have copy-catted, a few have outright ripped off my shock-n-awe package formats without any real understanding of the psychology behind it.)

I am also widely respected as "king of continuity", using "membership concept" to get consumers as well as businesspeople to agree to having their credit cards automatically charged for a pre-set amount each month, for bundled goods and services, typically in advance of delivery or use of those goods and services, thus creating stable and predictable income, blocking seduction by competitors, and increasing average retained customer value. We've done this with hair-cuts: a chain I helped launch, Kennedy's (KennedysBarberClubs.com) has, at this writing, over 4,000 members paying by the month, not by the haircut. Diana's Gourmet Pizzeria has done it with a pizza restaurant, per my model. The GKIC business that publishes my *No B.S. Marketing Letter*, other publications, and delivers online and seminar training to hundreds of thousands of entrepreneurs is entirely based on a membership/continuity model (DanKennedy.com).

For the life of me, I can't understand the paucity of upsells. This is one of the most easily understood Processes – *would you like fries with that?* – yet most businesses omit it from their Process Portfolio. I recently arrived at, checked in at the Omni at CNN Center in Atlanta, where a nice "Jr. Suite" had been reserved for me. And it was fine. But they weren't busy. Why not pitch me on upgrade to Luxury Suite if available, or a massage at the spa or in-room, or the CNN backstage tour or *something?* We KNOW FOR A FACT that no less than 5% to 20% of buyers of just about anything will say yes to an upsell, if made appealing, and especially if it's marginal increase in price. Same with tiered pricing. The last personal selling environment I was in, as a speaker, I offered three packages: 55% took the highest price, 35%

the middle, 10% the lowest. The amount of money that would have been left behind if there were only the two, my middle and low, *scary*. Further, the more affluent the consumer the more susceptible to tiers or upsells, especially if limited, because they respond well to exclusivity, they habitually buy the best options, and they have the ability to buy.

A few weeks back, we were out with friends at a high-end steakhouse, one in a chain. We all declined dessert. We were not invited to select a dessert to be nicely packaged to take home with us. Why on earth not? And what about pre-booking another evening, with some incentive to do so? When I placed my room service order for dinner at the Omni, no attempt was made to add a dessert or secure a breakfast order.

I'll tell you what it is. It is ignorance. Sloth. Often, the tactical procedure has been created, but there's no enforcement to speak of, so it gets done only by some employees, some of the time. And there's just no *hustle*. Years back, I was in a hotel, and got my boots shined at the lobby shoeshine stand. Guy asked how many nights I was staying. I said: two. He said: why don't you drop your other boots or shoes off anytime before I close today, I'll shine 'em up, and have room service bring 'em up to you in a bag first thing in the morning – you tell me the time. See, hustle. I asked him how that worked. He said he did about 30 to 40 pair of shoes that way, all assembly line in the back room when he closed up shop, gave the room service guys $1 a pair, plus most got tips when they delivered; he made an extra $150 to $200 a day. About $40,000.00 a year more than he would have otherwise. Said it put his kid through college. Hustle. It's unimaginable how much money all sorts of business let slip away, because they don't offer tiers of service, upsells, add-ons. If a shoe shine guy found $40,000.00 a year, how much might you find?

OFFER STRATEGY

Direct-response marketing is much about the offer – and one of the most common of all advertising and marketing mistakes is the utter absence of offer or a plain vanilla, ordinary offer.

Here's a terrific example from one of my newsletters, the *No B.S. Marketing to the Affluent Letter:*

You've seen this mansion on the HBO series ENTOURAGE, as home of its star, Vincent Chase and his hangers-on. It actually belonged to Sam Nazarian, CEO of the upscale hotel, resort and nightclub company SBE. It has 3 bedrooms, 5 baths, panoramic ocean views, a resort-style pool and spa area, a Hollywood Hills location. It was first put on the market for $18.5-million in 2009, and languished there, with no takers. Then *a major marketing re-boot*.

This time around, the $18-million mansion was bundled with a collection of exclusive premiums, including VIP guest privileges at all Nazarian hotels and clubs, catered house parties, hotel services and concierge services even including an on-call personal assistant – essentially making the house your personal resort. This is an Offer Strategy usually called Gift-With-Purchase. Estee Lauder is generally credited with inventing it for the department store cosmetic counter, where it is still the #1 "control cream" after all these years. But here it's not being used to sell a pile of wrinkle creams with free leopard tote back – it's driving the sale of an $18-million piece of real estate.

This listing/offer was NOT publicly advertised as luxury real estate – instead made known only to a select pool of privileged buyers given a personal access card with secret pass-codes to the listing's details and an online presentation. The property was sold for $17.9-million *in the first week*, breaking a local record for price per square foot.

What occurs to me: the real estate industry is horribly unimaginative. They ALL think "price" and "reducing price" (discounting) – when even with the most affluent consumers, the right bonus gifts can be much more persuasive. In this case, instead of reducing, reducing and reducing the price, to $15-million, $13-million, maybe less, the seller put in bonuses that won't cost more than that; will probably cost less; and create something truly unique that *no one else can have or replicate*, providing *unique experience*, bragging rights, exclusivity. Once a truly unique product/offer replaced just another hunk of exorbitantly priced luxury real estate, the way was cleared for a direct, targeted, efficient marketing campaign. The outcome: desired price and speed. This is a business model worth slowing down and thinking about, long and hard.

CELEBRITY STRATEGY

Some weeks, the Kardashians seem to own the entire newsstand rack. But celebrity has moved out of "movie magazines" long, long ago, to invade sports, business, finance and investment, and virtually every other category of commerce. A secret I teach is that the higher one's income, the more they are being paid for who they are – not what they do. The right "who-ing strategy" for the right market may incorporate and differently weight authority, credibility, expert status, key associations and other factors, but it will always incorporate celebrity in at least one if not two ways: (1) presenting yourself as a celebrity; (2) connecting yourself and your business, products or services with a celebrity or celebrities. Of course, the publishers of this book, Nick Nanton, Jack Dicks, and their agency, publishing enterprises and coaching are all about transforming you into a celebrity. They should be listened to on this subject. I have had 30 years' of extensive experience assisting small business and big corporate clients with obtaining affordable, effective celebrities for their advertising, marketing, seminars and conferences and even store and spa grand openings, and the list of entertainment, sports, business and political celebrities I've hired, booked and rented, obtained for clients, brought to the stage of our own GKIC events, and spoken on programs with repeatedly would fill a book – from Donald Trump (obtained for a client and appeared with myself) to Gene Simmons (KISS), Ivanka Trump, Adam West (Batman) and George Foreman (for GKIC events), and the list goes on and on.

If you study "marketing miracles" you find them celebrity driven far more often than not.

PRICE STRATEGY & PRICE *ELASTICITY* STRATEGY

I strongly recommend getting a copy of my book *No B.S. Price Strategy*. It summarizes and demonstrates many of the price strategies I've used personally and often use to dramatically and instantly multiply a client's income. Most people under-price and most improperly structure and present price vs. what would be most persuasive and effective with their clientele. I have probably created more wealth for more business owners by influencing their price strategy than by any other single means.

Underestimating the amount of price elasticity and the height of the price pyramid in a category is common failing. Gardner's Mattress thrives selling mattresses priced from $4,000.00 to $35,000.00, surrounded by over 100 stores selling at the national average of $600.00. Diana sells pizza at $22.00 to $38.00 despite a "2 for $10" shop a few steps away. I am routinely paid upwards from $100,000.00 plus royalties for ad copywriting projects – and there's a whole directory full of credentialed, experienced copywriters who will work for pennies or dimes on my dollars. There is, obviously, both Denny's and Starbucks, Kia and Lexus and Rolls-Royce, Motel 6 and Ritz-Carlton.

Most people handicap themselves with regard to price in four ways: one, their own self-sabotage and poor attitudes about price and misunderstanding of why and how money moves – which I explore in my book *No B.S. Wealth Attraction in the New Economy*. Two, their own poor selection of prospects, customers clients or patients, something explored in my book *No B.S. Marketing to the Affluent*. Three, weak price and price elasticity strategy. Four, sometimes, ineffective price *architecture*. As example of the latter, my client, VIE Partners, prices its expense reduction consulting services to major hospitals as a percentage of over-payment recapture and expense reduction rather than fee for service or hourly billing norms in consulting. Another example, already referenced here, is continuity in place of cafeteria pricing and pay as you use.

<u>NOT</u> IN CONCLUSION

There is a harmful tendency to confuse one's deliverables with one's business. This is a root cause of the poor question I get from so many, with increasing frequency: *how can I get "all this" done for me?….* and the whining complaint I hear as well: *I don't have the time for "all this"* – this marketing work, this study. Well, suck your thumb and settle for ordinary income. Those who get near the top of both the Income Pyramid and the Wealth Pyramid make a giant mental shift and have it govern their behavior: they decide their business IS marketing. It doesn't matter if the deliverable is pizza, dentistry, financial planning and investments, acne glop, consulting and copywriting, auto repair or zoo cleaning: those things are *not* the business. They are *not* the source of money. And no 'miracles' will come from the doing of them.

Therefore, this is NOT in conclusion, nor can any chapter in any book about marketing be a conclusion. Marketing is not something you learn – it is something you do. It shouldn't be something you delegate or outsource, unless you like working at the short end of the money stick. *Each and every day*, those rich by marketing, report to school and to work in their marketing department.

ABOUT DAN

Dan S. Kennedy is a multi-millionaire, serial entrepreneur, a sought after and exceptionally well-compensated marketing advisor and direct-response copywriter, popular speaker, and author of more than 20 business books including those in his popular No B.S. series, the most recent: No B.S. Grassroots Marketing for Local Businesses, No B.S. Trust-Based Marketing, and No B.S. Marketing to Leading-Edge Boomers and Seniors. His books are easily found at amazon.com or BN.com and available at all booksellers, and information is at NoBSBooks.com. Information about his newsletters and other resources at WeRecommendDan.com. Direct inquiries regarding his availability for speaking engagements, consulting or copywriting should be sent by fax to 602-269-3113.

CHAPTER 2

ARE YOU BORING AND BUGGING YOUR PROSPECTS WITH YOUR FOLLOW-UP?

HOW TO BE FUN AND ENTERTAINING INSTEAD

BY DAVID LINTON

I t's Monday morning, and you are going thru a pile of papers, hoping to find potential sales. On these papers are your notes and the contact information of an assortment of leads. All these folks contacted you sometime in the past, interested in what you sell. A couple of them called or emailed you just last week, and there are a bunch of "good ones"—leads that you have been working on for a while now that you just *know* will be deciding on something SOON. So you want to be sure to get thru them all this week so a big sale doesn't fall through the cracks.

In addition to the stack of papers with notes on them, you have a few folders in your outlook with the conversations of your most probable prospects. Oh, and don't forget the referral that some guy gave you last week—he told you his friend was in the market and was probably going to buy this week, so you need to call him right away or it could be too late. He gave you his card.... Where did you put it? Is it lost?

Well after spending all morning looking for that card, you decide to call the guy that gave you the lead and see if he can give you the contact information again 'cause you've lost the card.

He wasn't in, so you left a message for him to return your call. You have an hour before your afternoon appointment so you're going to see what you can do with the rest of your pending leads—before the week slips away and you don't get around to calling all of them—**again**.

So first on your list is Bob Garland. He has been on top of your list for a while because you need to call him at just the right time. You left him a voicemail last week just to check in with him and see if he needs anything else from you before he makes his final decision. This is going to be a BIG sale and you don't want to bug him again just yet, so put it to the side and let's start with #2.

#2 you don't feel like it's the right time to call just yet.

You call #3 and have a good chat. You write on your notes *"He's still deciding, and has my card, will call me when he makes a decision." (Call him in 2 weeks because he'll be buying soon).*

You manage to get thru the first 12 in your pile before it's time to head out for your appointment. Most of the rest of them were "still deciding". (Note to self: Next week—start at the bottom of the pile and work up.)

"STILL DECIDING"

Have you ever wondered, of all the people that you talk to, how many actually buy something—from you or anyone? When they tell you they are "still deciding," do they ever decide? The reality is that many of them are not only deciding what and from whom to buy, but they are also deciding if they are going to buy at all, and if so, when. They may have a problem to solve and a need for what you offer, but they have no idea what their options are or what the cost will be. The reason they contacted you was to find out the price and what is involved, to help them decide when to buy at all. Many times, the first visit is the beginning of the buying cycle, and it could be 9 months before they actually do anything.

Most salespeople treat everyone like a **NOW** customer, when, in reality, that only accounts for 10% of the people they interact with. The other 90% are "still deciding" what to buy and "still deciding" where to buy it and "still deciding" when to buy. For these, it's so very early in the buying cycle that most salespeople give up on them, thinking they never will buy.

So you probably spent half of all last week talking to people who were never going to buy right away anyway. Many will buy *someday* though, so the time spent last week was still worthwhile —**as long as they choose you** when they are finally ready to buy. This is a HUGE opportunity for you because all your competitors are going to give up on these people *waaaay* to soon. Warning: be careful not to bug and bore them with your follow-up communications or you will lose them forever. In this chapter I'm going to teach you how to follow-up in a fun and entertaining way so they like hearing from you instead of just pushing that "unsubscribe."

THE SHOPPING PROCESS

When a prospect talks to a salesperson, they usually tell him what they think they want. It doesn't matter if their budget is $100 or $100,000, the process is the same. They want to compare what you have to what they are looking for; sometimes they even have a sample proposal to compare yours with.

After visiting with you, they jot down the prices you quoted, ask for brochures (or that business card they say they will keep); then tell you they'll "think about it." This is the part of the process you see every day.

Here's what you DON'T see. They repeat the same process over and over with your competitors. Then they take all their newly collected brochures and prices to go home and forget everything all the salespeople told them and compare their notes and prices.

Then they conclude they can get the same quality thing, at a certain price, from any one of you.

So how to decide on who to buy from? Of course, YOU'RE the sales guy who told them *"you'd match or even beat any other quoted price, within the same quality range, and should they find something they like elsewhere, to bring you a sample proposal and you could certainly get them a comparable or a better price on the same quality thing or better."*

So, you are sure you have the deal in the bag—right? They will be talking to you again so you'll have an opportunity to close the deal before it is too late. Ask yourself this: do you sell to much more than 12-20% of the prospects you talk to? Does everyone call you before they buy from your competitor to at least give you another opportunity to get their business?

Well, let me let you in on a little secret I learned from one of my prospects. I used to own a flooring store, Casa Bella Home Solutions. When people would tell me they were "shopping around" I would tell them if they found something they liked elsewhere to bring in a sample, and I would find a comparable product and match or beat their price.

One day, a customer gave me some news I needed to hear (but I didn't like to hear). She told me that Tom at Brown-Vann Carpet One told her that he could get her something similar to mine, only at a better price, if only she'd bring him a sample. Then she visited Floor & Décor and Caroline told her the same thing, so did Wayne at Wayne's Carpet Plus. Even the kid at Lowes said that. (Although he had to read it out of the "How To Sell Flooring" manual they gave him last week when they moved him out of the plumbing section into flooring). Know that your competitors are also telling your prospect to call them before deciding—as they may be able to match **your** quote.

So, what about the all the time spent listening to their plans and wants, recommending a particular solution, going through all the steps necessary to figure out a quote for them and presenting it to them in a manner conducive to making the sale? Do you think that 3 months from now, when they are getting closer to the purchase, they will remember all the time you spent with them? They'll likely remember spending a day looking around but it is doubtful they will remember much, if any, of yours' or any other conversation. They will have a few notes they took, but they won't remember you. They will be spending another day shopping, so all of that time you spent was essentially wasted. To put it differently YOU WASTED HALF OF LAST WEEK, THIS WEEK, AND EVERY WEEK. And there is nothing that can be done about it because you never know which half you are wasting.

Actually *there is one thing that can be done about it:* You can send your prospects frequent emails pointing out all the different reasons that choosing you will benefit them. And mix it up with some non-email communications so they are getting it from different media and therefore, pay more attention to it. If they visit 5 people today, and 9 months later they are ready to buy, and everybody forgets about them except you, they will forget everybody except you. I assure you that no one else even sent them a thank-you note after their visit and then kept in touch with them for the past 9 months—*except for a few annoying phone calls they quickly disconnect from because they are too busy to talk*, and your prospect hasn't even thought further about making a decision anyway.

Your business will increase significantly if you put a follow-up system in place to nurture potential buyers who are not yet ready to buy. Think about how much time is wasted and money lost with all the prospects who end up buying somewhere else? Think of all the sales you almost had "in the bag," but the prospect wasn't ready to buy just then, and then when they were ready to buy they forgot about you and called somebody else.

How much do you make from an average sale? What if you could attach a dollar amount to the time you spent with people who ultimately forget about you and bought elsewhere? What if you could start selling to even just 20% of the prospects you talked to but then bought from your competition? How much money have you been losing—money that would have been yours had you effectively followed-up?

A study done by the Association of Sales Executives revealed that **81% of all sales happen on or after the fifth contact.** So implementing a good follow-up system could easily double your sales within a year.

DON'T BE BORING AND BUGGING

One of the biggest mistakes people make when creating a follow-up sequence of emails is being boring. Think about it. How many boring emails do you delete every day without even reading them?

The other HUGE mistake many salespeople make is bugging their prospects with messages like:

"Have you had a chance to review my proposal?"

"Did I answer all your questions, or is there anything I could provide that would help with your decision?"

"Are you ready to move ahead with…?"

"Did you get my last email?"

As marketing director for Everlast Epoxy Flooring Company, I had to figure out a solution to this problem. We manufacture a commercial epoxy flooring so you can imagine how boring our follow-up emails could be. It often takes a long time for someone to buy after they first call us because people like to research building materials while their project is still in the planning stages, and they usually haven't even started building yet. So I had to come up with a follow-up sequence to keep them interested all the way through the building process until they were finally ready to buy the floors.

I needed to find a way to effectively send frequent emails about our flooring without boring our prospects to delete. I had to think like my customer. What if I got an email that read: *"David, Everlast Floor provides a bonding and strength greater than the cohesive strength of concrete in tension and shear. The durability and abrasion resistance far surpasses that of dense concrete so Everlast Floor will maintain its original beauty for years to come. And Everlast Floor is a monolithic, resin-rich, troweled-on system that forms a physical bond between the material and the surface it is being applied to and vulcanizes them together. The compound made is so tightly bonded together that corrosive materials cannot penetrate to begin the deterioration process. Everlast Floor is not adhered to the floor, rather it is the adhesive. Under stress conditions, the concrete will break instead of your epoxy floor's bond. So call us at (800) 708-9870 when you are ready to purchase your flooring. Sincerely – Everlast Epoxy"*

Boy, how many times do you have to mash that delete button just to wake yourself up after reading that? I'm not a big fan of boring my prospects, so I decided to send them cartoons instead. I put together a sequence of cartoons that each point out a different benefit of our floor in a fun way. Those emails are waaay more fun to see, and the chance of them getting opened and read is 10 times better. Plus when my prospects get their next email from me, they will open it because they will expect another fun cartoon!

So after 9 months of getting a different cartoon about Everlast Floor every 3 weeks, which floor do you think they will think of? Do you think they will remember ANY of the others? Sure, that doesn't guarantee the sale, but is sure does guarantee another shot! If the cartoons are done right, they "drip" on your prospects repeatedly, each time instilling in their minds another reason to do business with you—in a fun and entertaining way.

The cartoons were so much fun and work so well, I decided to make them for other businesses too. So I got involved with CartoonMarketing.com and EmailDripCRM.

EmailDripCRM is a software that keeps track of all your prospects' contact information, keeps them segmented as needed, stores your notes about each prospect, and automatically sends out your cartoon emails at scheduled intervals. Because it is cloud based, you can view your contacts information anywhere, even on your mobile—and—so you won't lose track of your referral next time. You can even add contacts while on the go!

CartoonMarketing.com has a huge gallery of business cartoons. You're sure to find some that will work for you, or we can design a custom campaign just for your business.

So now you can break up your sales message into a series of emails, each pointing out a different benefit of doing business with you, and set them up to be sent out 1-3 weeks apart over a period of 3-9 months. AND your prospects will enjoy getting our emails because they know there will be a cartoon inside.

See the software at www.EmailDrip.com. As a special bonus for getting this book, I will give you a **FREE Cartoon** you can use for your business. Get your FREE cartoon at www.CartoonMarketing.com/MarketingBook.

Lowest Bidder

ABOUT DAVID

David Linton lives with his wife and three children in Lake City, Florida–home of Mountaintop Ministries Worldwide, a Holy Ghost filled Christian non-denominational outreach ministry they are proud supporters of. (Visit www.mtmww.com for more info and to watch services online ALWAYS FOR FREE.)

David is a leading authority on business sales and marketing. His specialty is creating fun and entertaining marketing campaigns that keep people interested all through the buying phase and compels them to buy.

David Linton is the founder of EmailDrip.com Inc., whose two key products are: EmailDripCRM and CartoonMarketing.com. He also creates the proprietary cartoon email campaigns for EmailDripCRM users.

David is author of *Quit Bidding, Start Selling - How to take your subcontract construction business from zero to two million in two years*.

David Linton is also currently the marketing director for Everlast Epoxy Flooring Company (www.EverlastEpoxy.com). David's marketing has landed them contracts for projects in facilities such as Kesselring Site (Atomic Power Lab) operated by the USA Navy, NavConBrig Military prison in Charleston SC, the Hoover Dam, the Grand Canyon National Park, Augusta National Golf Club (hosts the Masters Tournament), the Baltimore Orioles, United States military hospital in Afghanistan, Elgin Air Force Base, Peterson Air Force Base, Auburn University, University of Maryland, Utah Valley State College, Washington State University, Sony Pictures in Hollywood CA, Maryland Correctional Institute, Pennsylvania Department of Corrections and South Carolina Department of Corrections.

David's marketing has also generated direct response from Sandals Resorts in Jamaica, Norwegian Cruise Line, Halliburton, the Afghan National Army, the Cleveland Cavaliers and NASA.

David's Everlast Floor has been featured on the DIY Network.

www.EmailDripCRM.com

A degree in Computer Geek University is not needed to use EmailDripCRM's user-friendly web-based system. With a few clicks of the mouse you can easily add contacts, segment lists, send emails, browse through the massive newsletter template gallery, and create opt-in forms for your website. It's easy as 1-2-3 to plug your leads into an 18-email automated follow-up sequence, a 5-email lost customer reactivation sequence—whatever sequence you need!

EmailDripCRM is home of the "**One Click Direct Response.**" The caption of your cartoon or the additional text underneath can have a "click here" that will take your reader directly to your website or order page.

EmailDripCRM's easy to view and use calendar will show you monthly, weekly, and daily views. Making appointments is simple; they can even sync with the contact record. Make and change appointments with easy-to-use 'drag and drop' functionality.

www.CartoonMarketing.com

Implementing an email cartoon campaign is easy because we've done the work for you. We've created effective cartoons for practically every business and industry. CartoonMarketing.com has a huge gallery of cartoons to choose from for the perfect email campaign. Drawn exclusively for EmailDripCRM users, designed to motivate your customers to buy from you.

Special offer just for reading my book: I'll give you a FREE cartoon for YOUR business. AND the cartoon is YOURS TO KEEP forever. Get it at www.CartoonMarketing.com/MarketingBook.

CHAPTER 3

NO TEST DRIVE NEEDED:

GET CUSTOMERS READY TO BUY *TODAY* THROUGH EDUCATIONAL MARKETING

BY GREG ROLLETT

I f you are like most entrepreneurs, experts, authors or business owners, the concept of hard selling is not an attractive one. In fact, you probably find ways to spend your time doing anything *but* cold calling, direct selling or getting on the phone to try and close a prospect.

I know I have had my share of "working distractions"—from checking Facebook posts to looking at website statistics to checking my email for the umpteenth time. And no matter how many times we perform these activities, no money is going to be deposited into our back accounts.

And that is not good for business.

The good thing is that with the tools and information available to you today, you don't need to spend every minute of every day selling. I'm not saying you do not have to sell at all, because you do. But using a concept called Educational Marketing allows you to begin to attract and position the right type of client or customer into your business; this ultimately makes the selling part easy because they already sold themselves on your products or services through educational pieces (created to paint a picture of what you do and how it helps individuals like them).

WHAT IS EDUCATIONAL MARKETING?

Educational Marketing is the process of creating educational pieces of content that move a prospect into a position of realizing *you* are the ultimate expert who can help solve their problem.

Think about your best clients or customers. Who are they? Where did they come from? How did they make the decision to purchase from you?

Most likely it was because they were educated that you were the best solution. They had information on who you were, what you did and how you can help them.

Imagine that you were a car dealer and had 2 potential customers on your lot. The first customer was a first-time car buyer and wants to test drive 10 or more cars before talking it over, asking more questions and then price checking with your competition.

The second customer comes into your lot, already educated that you have a red pickup truck, 2 doors, with power windows, 6-disc CD changer, 4-wheel drive and all the other bells and whistles. They also know the price, have been pre-approved by their bank for a loan and are ready to walk out with the keys in a matter of minutes.

Which customer do you wish you had more of, walking into your business every day, attracted to your business and your products and services?

I hope you said customer number 2.

In this scenario, your educational and informational pieces, from the web, print, direct mail, or your phone sales team has educated your customer so they can easily make an informed decision. They have already sold themselves as to which product they want. The customer had a problem and educated themselves on a solution. The education they found through the above sources led them to create their own opinions and come to the conclusion that you were the solution to their problem.

This empowers the customer and makes them feel important, comforted and confident in their decision. They were not sold to; they made their own informed, educated decision.

When done correctly, this is a very powerful distinction and has a profound impact on your business.

USING EDUCATION IN YOUR MARKETING

Many experts and entrepreneurs think they are using educational marketing, especially online. They have created a website that is supposed to attract and educate individuals coming to their website. It is filled with features and benefits, services offered and potentially even some testimonials and case studies of work they have done.

But most do not truly educate and help the individual move closer to finding a solution to their problem, and most of all, it does not move them closer to knowing that their real solution to their problem is you!

If you know the importance of educational marketing you might have special reports, white papers, eZines and newsletters, videos or other forms of media that were designed to give valuable information to someone that is unfamiliar with you and what you do.

Where these media pieces fail to become truly effective pieces of consumer education is in their ability for the reader to draw the conclusion that they are now more educated about the problem they are having, the opportunity to find a solution and that you are indeed the right expert or business they must do business with in order to get the solution they desire.

Thus the only three things you want your marketing resources to do are:

1. To attract your exact target market and reveal the problem they are having in such a way that they feel, deep down, that you know their problem better than they do.

2. To reveal an opportunity to stop the problem they are currently having and then teach them how to do so,

3. To educate the reader on how *you* are the only solution, the ultimate expert, that can truly help them get the results they desire.

Let's take a look at how successful businesses are using these strategies today to educate their clients on how they are the clear choice of a solution to their problems.

THE ONLINE MARKETER

Today you cannot look anywhere online without seeing educational marketing at work. A select few are much better than others at truly educating their marketplace, making them aware of the problems they are having and educating them on the solution they are presenting to fix that problem.

One of the leaders in this space is Rich Schefren from Strategic Profits. Rich has been a successful entrepreneur in the men's retail and hypnosis center business and upon selling his hypnosis centers, found his way into online marketing. When he launched his coaching and consulting company, Strategic Profits, Rich created a manifesto called "The Internet Business Manifesto" which was read almost overnight by millions of struggling online marketers who all shared the problem of "opportunity seeking" and were not business building.

This manifesto served as a textbook for many online marketers, while educating and identifying with the readers Rich identified with them by sharing his story of "opportunity seeking" online. Then he shared the opportunity, which was to overcome the "shiny object syndrome" by going from tactic to tactic. Next he revealed the benefits of becoming a strategic entrepreneur. Finally through the manifesto, Rich positioned himself as the ultimate expert in this arena, by virtue that no one else was talking about these ideas, these problems and offering a clear solution, backed by proof, case studies and his own success. After reading you were certain that Rich was the clear choice, the clear expert and had the solution to help you alleviate your online business problems.

Today Rich has taken his manifesto and now uses the same principles in an online webinar. The entire 2-hour presentation is filled with education, strategically positioned to attract the right kind of client, revealing the problem that this right kind of client is having and then using proof, experience and marketing to reveal he is the ultimate expert and solution.

In your marketing, you want to model a system like this. Create free reports or webinars that are educational marketing pieces and not just a report to have a report, or have a webinar to have a webinar. Always use these marketing pieces to educate your prospects using the 3-step approach.

THE PR AGENCY

The Dicks + Nanton Celebrity Branding Agency is a shiny example of using educational marketing to build their client base and attract the right kind of client into their business. When they began the business, Nick Nanton and JW Dicks wrote a very educational and informational Best-Selling Book, *Celebrity Branding You*. To this day, the book is used as a tool to educate their market about their 5-step branding process to help you become a celebrity in their marketplace.

Each of the 5 steps relate to a service they offer, from helping authors become Best-Sellers to getting experts and entrepreneurs featured on major TV and print outlets to using media like branded films. All of these are presented as problems and then opportunities throughout the book to help teach authors, experts and entrepreneurs to grow their brand. They knew that by educating their clients on the benefits and effects of celebrity branding, they would be positioning themselves as the experts and authorities on the subject. And it was all done through a well-written and better positioned book.

Today, along with the book, Nick and JW are using white papers and reports that relate to each segment of their business that go right through the 3-steps in the educational marketing process. For their book publishing business they have created a report on the "7 Myths of Publishing." This report overcomes the 7 biggest objections people have in joining their publishing company. The report magnetically attracts the right kind of author, talks about some of their fears and doubts about the publishing process and offers a clear, expert solution, with proof and examples of others just like them that have benefited from co-authoring a Best-Selling book.

Another report on "Branded Films" has helped to develop an entirely new brand, Celebrity Films. This report again fulfills the same three requirements of great educational marketing and those who read the report and then contact the agency are already sold on the process—they need the solution in order to grow their business. That is very powerful and makes the job of selling much, much easier.

THE FINANCIAL ADVISOR

The financial services industry is very competitive and people are more skeptical than ever on whom to select to manage their money. This brings a big problem to those in this industry to build trust and grow their clientele. The best financial planners know the power of educational marketing: to position them as the go-to expert, someone that can be trusted and someone that you truly would like to do business with.

Stephen Lomsdalen from Scottsdale, AZ, is one such advisor doing this successfully in his market. Stephen has created a book of his own, *The 3 Wall Street Myths That Could Destroy Your Retirement Dreams*. Just from the title of the book he is attracting a certain type of market, those about to retire and who are worried about the current state of Wall Street.

On the inside of the book, Stephen talks about the challenges and fears his market is currently having. He relates to them in a very intimate way, painting a picture of their feelings and insecurities about the future of their life after retirement. He also shares the 3 strategies that this age-class has been taught and told over the years that are not accurate and relevant to their retirement plans today.

By the end of the book, the only thing you want to do is pick up the phone and call Stephen for a consultation. This is very powerful marketing, and was all created through an educational piece, which taught his market about their problems and presented solutions so they can come up with their own logical conclusions on how to proceed.

YOUR EDUCATIONAL MARKETING ROADMAP

Now that you have seen some examples and have an idea of how to use educational marketing in your business, it's time to create your own educational pieces. This begins by identifying who the ideal person it is that you want to attract. Who is most likely to buy your products and services? Who do you want coming in to buy your products and services?

Once you've identified the "who," you need to look at the deep-down problem the market is having. What keeps them up at night? What would make their life better? The best place to find this information is to ask your current customer base. Why did they buy your products or services? What solution were they really looking for? Why did they choose you and not someone else?

Now we have our market and we know their problems. Our next step is to map out that problem. What feelings are associated with their problem? What is going on in their mind? How is it affecting their day-to-day decisions? How is it affecting their income? Their relationships? Their family? Start writing these answers down, as they will become the beginning of your educational marketing piece. Talk with the market; make them understand that you know what they are going through, and that they are not alone.

Next you need to start presenting the solution. How can their life improve? Paint the picture of what life can look like once they take action on a solution. Begin to educate them about the solution. Teach them what can happen with the right solution. Present the solution using logical steps, in a do-this and then do-that fashion.

All along you want to integrate proof, case studies and reasons why you are the expert they need in their life. At the end, offer your solution. Give them a place to take the next step.

This entire process can be done in any kind of media—it happens on infomercials selling blenders and Ginsu knives and on webinars, in newsletters, online product launches, books and even through email sequences. Just remember to *create a purpose* with your marketing pieces. No more free reports to have a report. Give your marketing purpose so your prospects are educated and one step away from doing business with you.

ABOUT GREG

Greg Rollett, the ProductPro, is a best-selling author and online marketing expert who works with authors, experts, entertainers, entrepreneurs and business owners all over the world to help them share their knowledge and change the lives and businesses of others. After creating a successful string of his own educational products, Greg began helping others in the production and marketing of their own products.

Greg is a front-runner in utilizing the power of social media, direct response marketing and customer education to drive new leads and convert those leads into long-standing customers and advocates.

Previous clients include Coca-Cola, Miller Lite, Warner Bros and Cash Money Records, as well as hundreds of entrepreneurs and small-business owners. Greg's work has been featured on FOX News, ABC, and the Daily Buzz. Greg has written for Mashable, the Huffington Post, AOL, AMEX's Open Forum and more.

Greg loves to challenge the current business environments that constrain people to working 12-hour days during the best portions of their lives. By teaching them to leverage technology and the power of information, Greg loves helping others create freedom businesses that allow them to generate income, make the world a better place and live a radically ambitious lifestyle in the process.

A former touring musician, Greg is highly sought after as a speaker, having appeared on stages with former Florida Gov. Charlie Crist, best-selling authors Chris Brogan and Nick Nanton, as well as at events such as Affiliate Summit.

If you would like to learn more about Greg and how he can help your business, please contact him directly at greg@productprosystems.com or by calling his office at 877.897.4611.

You can also download a free report on how to create your own educational products at www.productprosystems.com.

CHAPTER 4

THE MIRACLE SALES POWER OF YOUR IRRESTIBLE OFFER!

BY JW DICKS AND NICK NANTON

YOU HAVE THREE SECONDS!

Just three seconds. Can your marketing sales piece deliver in that amount of time?

Your problem is…*it has to.*

Just as the door-to-door salesman of days gone by had to shove his foot in the door to stop the homeowner from slamming the door in his face, you need to find the exact right device to stop your potential prospect from slamming his mind shut to what *you* have to say.

That device is your **Irresistible Offer**. It's the secret to enticing people into listening to your marketing message. And if it's crafted in the right way, you'll find you don't have to shove your foot in anyone's mental door —potential buyers will gladly open their minds to hear more about what you're selling.

DEFINING THE IRRESISTIBLE OFFER

An Irresistible Offer, simply put, *is a way of defining your product or service with an offer that clearly creates an impactful and credible return on investment which is almost impossible to turn down.*

The truth is, it all comes down to "I will give you this…in return for that." No matter what your product or service is, it <u>all</u> starts with an offer—and if the offer isn't compelling, it ends there. If the offer is "irresistible," you can build an entire business on the back of that offer.

Without the irresistible offer, you're left with meaningless marketing that can't make a sale.

Remember: *nothing happens in any business or profession without an offer.* Many business and professional practices forget that basic fact, which is why they fail miserably. Too many advertising campaigns try to be overly clever, way too subtle or just lazily piggyback on something more successful. In the process, they forget to actually *sell* their product or service, hard as that is to believe. "Ask for the order" is the old sales mantra that still reverberates to this day no matter what your business or profession is.

Now, if nothing happens without an offer, *a whole lot happens with an Irresistible Offer.* It's the offer on steroids—it powers it up and knocks it out of the park.

DEFINING YOUR PRODUCT OR SERVICE

The first step to creating your Irresistible Offer is to ask three important questions about what you're selling. This is the place to be completely honest, because, if you're not, you're only fooling yourself – and that's going to be a very costly deception. Your Irresistible Offer will be flawed and its impact will be blunted.

- **QUESTION #1: WHAT ARE YOU SELLING AND WHAT'S YOUR PRICE?**

This is obviously the foundation of your Irresistible Offer, so it's of critical importance. Do you know the value exchange price for whatever you're providing the buyer with? Is what you're providing something they'll feel good about buying at that price, or will they feel suckered? The knowledge of understanding value exchange when setting price is very important.

Because price is part of the foundation for your irresistible offer, you need to make sure you have set the price for an amount that will be acceptable to the customer and will stand up to the prospect for the value of what he is getting. Here is where your basic believability lies. You don't charge a hundred dollars for a cheeseburger and another fifty bucks for the French fries, unless inflation has taken a real ugly turn by the time you read this. So review this basic part of the Irresistible Offer, make sure you're offering appropriate quality and quantity for the price and, if you're not, rethink either product or price. If the two don't tilt to the favor of the buyer you won't make the sale.

- **QUESTION #2: WHY SHOULD THEY LISTEN TO YOU?**

We've already touched on the idea of credibility—now let's go further into the subject. A crucial component of making any sale is creating a bond of *trust*. Simply put, people have to believe what you're saying is the truth. Raising suspicions is the last thing you want to do. So think about whether what you're offering appears too good to be true. Does it seem ridiculous at face value that you can deliver what you're saying you can deliver?

If so, people will think there's a catch to your deal—and, worse, you might be trying to trick them in some way. And remember, it doesn't even matter if you *can* deliver what you're promising; if people *think* you can't, it's going to hurt your offer.

You're especially vulnerable to this kind of doubt if you have little to no track record as of yet and people just don't know who you are or what your capabilities are. For instance, if Coke or Pepsi comes out and says their soft drinks can now cure cancer, many people might actually believe the claim, because they assume Coke or Pepsi couldn't make that kind of claim if it wasn't true.

If some outfit called Acme Cola, however, made that claim, nobody would buy it. Not only would nobody believe it cured cancer—they'd be afraid of the stuff eating through the lining of their stomachs, just because they never heard of the company.

When Burger King told consumers "Have It Your Way," it was an easily verifiable (and, at the time, irresistible!) offer. Same thing with Domino's 30-minutes-or-less pizza delivery promise, especially since it was backed with a discount if the pizza came late. Make sure your offer also has back-up that builds believability.

- **QUESTION #3: WHERE'S THE BEEF?**

One of the great fast food ad campaigns of all time was for the Wendy's chain. In the commercial, a little old lady stood at the counter of a rival burger joint, eyeing her microscopic hamburger patty, and yelled, "WHERE'S THE BEEF?"

In terms of your Irresistible Offer, "Where's the beef?" translates into "Where's the benefit for your buyer?" One of the biggest secrets of successful marketing is to clearly understand that people aren't really buying the product or service that you're selling. No, they're buying the *benefit* of that product or service.

Why do you buy an Infiniti instead of a Honda Civic? They're both cars and they'll both get you to where you want to go. The reason you pay a lot more for the Infiniti is that it provides a lot more benefits—more prestige, more features, a smoother drive, etc. And, if you'll notice, that's what their marketing zeroes in on. The Civic, on the other hand, will advertise the fact that it's economical and reliable, because those are its main benefits to the consumer.

Another big marketing secret comes into play here—people buy based more on emotions than logic, even though most of them will deny it after the fact. That's why most of the car commercials you'll see focus on making the vehicle look as "cool" as possible with big budget effects that have nothing to do with the actual product they're selling.

And that's why this third question is the most important. The first two require logic-based questions, but this is the question that drills deeper into the real appeal of your product or service. Remember, though, you still need the logic-based answers to the first two questions to balance your Irresistible Offer—because you always need a combination of both heart and head to effectively sell anything.

Now…let's find out how to bring that combination to life.

THE THREE INGREDIENTS OF YOUR IRRESISTIBLE OFFER

Just as there are three questions you must answer *before* formulating your Irresistible Offer, there are three ingredients you must put *into* it.

Before we explain those ingredients, a little more about what The Irresistible Offer is all about.

- It should be THE STARTING POINT of all your marketing. Everything will spring from your "Irresistible Offer." It won't be used as an afterthought on your marketing materials. It will lead the charge, not bring up the rear.

- An Irresistible Offer goes beyond a "New and Improved," "Big Sale," "Special Offer' mentality. These are well-worn gimmicks slapped on top of marketing to try and get more people in the door, kind of like a new coat of paint that's quickly applied to make a shabby apartment look instantly better. These gimmicks come and go, while the Irresistible Offer remains at the center of how you market.

- The Irresistible Offer also usually differs from a USP (Unique Selling Proposition). For example, Avis Rent-A-Car's famous line, "We Try Harder," is a USP, not an Irresistible Offer. "We Try Harder" indicates how Avis differs from the competition, but it's certainly nothing that makes you want to buy from Avis at that moment. Sometimes the USP can be the same as the Irresistible Offer—in Domino's case, the 30-minutes-Or-Less promises provides both functions—but, in many cases, it's not. However, the USP is a vital part of the Irresistible Offer.

Now, keeping all that in mind, here are the three ingredients that must be a part of every Irresistible Offer:

INGREDIENT #1: OFFER A UNIQUE DEAL THAT IS CLEAR, CREDIBLE AND ANSWERS WHY

Form and function work hand-in-hand to create the biggest impact.

That means you must work to craft your Irresistible Offer into the best possible and powerful *statement*. That statement should include the following facts:

- What you're selling

- What's the benefit to the buyer

- Why the offer is credible, i.e. why people should trust you

As you might remember, all of the needed information springs from those three questions we had you answer in the previous section.

Now, just stringing that information together isn't really going to do the job. If Federal Express said, "We're going to deliver your package by the next day at an affordable price so you can make sure it gets to where it needs to go in time, and if it doesn't, we'll refund your money," there's really not much of a chance anybody would've taken the time to read all that, let alone absorb the message.

Which is why they came up with, "When it absolutely, positively has to be there overnight" instead, one of the all-time great ad slogans.

Here are the elements they used to craft that slogan, which you should use to craft yours:

- **BE CLEAR**

There is no room for ambiguity or interpretation in an Irresistible Offer. Again, people have to muddle through millions of marketing messages a year; if you make them work too hard to figure something out, they're just going to go on with their lives. Clarity is all-important—it cuts through the clutter and tells the prospect exactly what he or she needs to know.

- **BE SIMPLE**

This goes hand-in-hand with the "clear" directive. Keep your language simple and easy-to-understand. You don't need to send someone to the dictionary to figure out what you're trying to say. Although if you actually get someone to go find one, that's a pretty impressive feat!

THE MIRACLE SALES POWER OF YOUR IRRESTIBLE OFFER!

- **BE BRIEF**

Compare the two Federal Express slogan examples used earlier. One took 9 words to make its point and the other took 37. Guess which one's a whole lot better?

- **BE DIRECT**

Cut right to the chase and say what you have to say. There's no need for embellishment or symbolism—using those kinds of things flies right in the face of the preceding three pieces of advice.

And also spend some time studying effective advertising slogans to see how they use a minimum of language to achieve maximum impact—in some cases, without even using real words.

For example, everybody remember what Campbell's Soup is? Yep, it's "Mmm, mmm, Good." Now, try finding "Mmm" in the dictionary. All you'll find is that it's an abbreviation of Member of the Order of the Military Merit (as you can tell, we sent ourselves to the dictionary!).

INGREDIENT #2: MAKE IT BELIEVABLE

One semi-famous marketer once put an ad in the newspaper with a headline that read, "What if I offered you $1000 for every dollar you gave me?" No one responded. Why? Because it was completely unbelievable!

Grandiose claims without proof won't get you the sales you want. So how *do* you demonstrate to your potential customer that you can be trusted, and that your Irresistible Offer is for real?

Every offer has its own ways to establish credibility. But there are basically three main methods to bring believability to your sales pitch:

- **USE TESTIMONIALS**

Valid, verifiable third-party testimonials go a long way towards demonstrating that people use your product or service and are happy with it. It's why companies hire celebrities to both appear in and do voiceovers for their commercials—the public already knows them and presumably, likes them. In your case, real consumers of what you're selling are probably the best testimonials you'll get, unless you can corral an expert in the field you're selling in.

There are other abstract ways to use testimonials directly in your Irresistible Offer. Remember the old commercials that would say "9 out of 10 doctors prefer…?" Of course, when you are using that kind of language, you should make sure you have the research available to back it up. And speaking of research…

• USE RESEARCH

Do you have scientific studies or tests that prove your product or service is superior to the rest? Does it effectively do what it's supposed to do 100% of the time and are there facts you can cite to prove it? Technical research that's credible and backs up your claims in a compelling manner can make a huge difference in establishing trust.

Think of the car commercials that state that one model has the best safety track record - or another model gets the most miles to the gallon. They base these statements on independent studies they can cite in the very small print in their marketing.

And of course, you can create your own research-based proof. Pepsi almost finally overtook Coke in the cola wars a while back, simply by doing "The Pepsi Challenge." They would go to a mall or other public place, have someone drink an unlabeled cup of Coke and an unlabeled cup of Pepsi and reveal which one they liked better. The proof was right there on camera—most people liked Pepsi better. The impact was huge. And it can be huge for you, if the numbers are on your side and you have a compelling way to present them.

• USE THE FACTS

Let's say you're selling gold. If gold prices are on the upswing, you just have to reference that trend. Let's say you're selling a non-stock market-based investment product. If the Dow Jones is on the downswing, use that fact to your advantage.

Even more instructive is watching any sort of political advertisement—you'll see a whole lot of facts. They may be used in a misleading way (which is why most of these ads don't have a lot of credibility going for them), but they're still facts.

If your offer is based in facts or a reality that almost everyone is aware of, this can be a potent form of "proof" indeed. For example, back in 1974, the MGM movie studio put out a compilation film of all the greatest moments from its musicals of the 30s, 40s and 50s.

Nobody thought anyone would actually go see it—the original movies had already been played on TV over and over for twenty-plus years.

However, since it was released on the heels of Watergate and Vietnam, the tagline for "That's Entertainment" was simply, "Boy. Do We Need It Now." The film was a huge smash and spawned two sequels.

INGREDIENT #3: CREATE A GREAT DEAL

Your Irresistible Offer must signal that the customer is going to get a high "Return On Investment" for their purchase. In other words, he or she must think you're giving a lot of bang for their buck. The ROI does not have to be cash but it must be a return that people understand has value to them and it has to be more than the value they are paying to make it irresistible.

And this means a genuinely good value. When we discussed the "Big Sale" and "New and Improved" types of marketing gimmicks, they're usually used to disguise the fact that the ROI isn't really all that great on the product or service. Cheesy attention-grabbers only work in the very short-term and often leave customers with a bad taste in their mouths.

If you actually are offering a great value, you don't have to resort to gimmicks. If the value is real, you've placed yourself in a good position for repeat sales from the same buyers. If it isn't, you'll have a big problem with your next marketing moves.

PUTTING YOUR IRRESISTIBLE OFFER INTO ACTION

Now it's time to put our three ingredients together. You should tackle them in the order we've discussed:

- Ingredient #1 - create the language that makes your unique deal clear, credible and answers why

- Ingredient #2 - put in the elements of believability that will seal that great deal of yours with your prospects

- Ingredient #3 - create your high-ROI deal that offers maximum benefits

If you've done your work well, you will cut through the clutter and pique your potential customer's interest. If you structured your deal so that it contains enough value for that customer, you've made a sale.

Let's revisit the film, "That's Entertainment," to see just how they made all this happen with a film that was, again, composed entirely of old movie clips. First of all, they made it a high value deal by putting together the greatest song-and-dance sequences from the greatest musicals and filmed new introductions to them with giant stars like Fred Astaire, Bing Crosby and Frank Sinatra.

Second of all, they came up with that great message, "Boy. Do We Need It Now," which hit the American public where they lived at that moment in history. And finally, their believability factor was easily off the charts since everyone was already familiar with these classic films and knew they were great.

But how did audiences connect with the film? Well, first they saw that tagline and liked the fact that someone was offering them some relief from the horrible headlines of the day. Second, they saw that a big famous movie studio, MGM, was behind the project—that provided the credibility. And third, they checked out the value—which stars and classic movies were represented in "That's Entertainment?" Pretty much all of them…an amazing value for audiences of the time.

Which is why there were two sequels; MGM continued to put their Irresistible Offer to work and so can you! Just follow these proven Steps to Success with your Irresistible Offer:

Step One: Create your Irresistible Offer

Step Two: Present that offer to an Interested Target Market

Step Three: Continue to keep their interest with more targeted Irresistible Offers

We've already covered **Step One** in detail; **Step Two** will be obvious to anyone who understands niche marketing. You don't try to sell anti-wrinkle cream to teenagers and you don't try to sell acne medicine to senior citizens. Whatever you're selling, you should find the crowd who will be the most responsive to your Irresistible Offer *and find the best way to reach them*.

Finally, **Step Three** is where you can make the most money. It's much easier to market to existing customers than to create new ones—and also a lot more affordable. Just as popular movies spawn sequels and popular TV shows spawn spin-offs, you can keep your current customers' interest by selling more stuff to them. It could be a new product for the same market or it could be a more premium version of the one you're already selling. The sky's the limit.

As we noted, your Irresistible Offer should be your "foot in the door" of anyone you're selling to. It should be something that should register immediately with your potential customer and make them consider buying from you in a serious manner. Make it a believable, high-value and carefully crafted message, and your Irresistible Offer will be just the beginning of many profitable years of business.

ABOUT JW

JW Dicks, Esq., is America's foremost authority on using personal branding for business development. He has created some of the most successful brand and marketing campaigns for business and professional clients to make them the Credible Celebrity Expert in their field and build multi-million-dollar businesses using their recognized status.

JW Dicks has started, bought, built, and sold a large number of businesses over his 39-year career and developed a loyal international following as a business attorney, author, speaker, consultant, and business expert's coach. He not only practices what he preaches by using his strategies to build his own businesses, he also applies those same concepts to help clients grow their business or professional practice the way he does.

JW has been extensively quoted in such national media as *USA Today, Wall Street Journal, Newsweek, Inc.* magazine, Forbes.com, CNBC.Com, and Fortune *Small business*. His television appearances include ABC, NBC, CBS and FOX affiliate stations around the country. He is the resident branding expert for Fast Company's internationally syndicated blog and is the publisher of Celebrity Expert Insider, a monthly newsletter targeting business- and brand-building strategies.

JW has written over 22 books, including numerous best-sellers, and has been inducted into the National Academy of Best Selling Authors. JW is married to Linda, his wife of 39 years, and they have two daughters, two granddaughters and two Yorkies. JW is a 6th generation Floridian and splits time between his home in Orlando and his beach house on the Florida west coast.

ABOUT NICK

An Emmy Award-Winning Director and Producer, Nick Nanton, Esq., is known as the Top Agent to Celebrity Experts around the world for his role in developing and marketing business and professional experts, through personal branding, media, marketing and PR to help them gain credibility and recognition for their accomplishments. Nick is recognized as the nation's leading expert on personal branding as *Fast Company* magazine's Expert Blogger on the subject and lectures regularly on the topic at at major universities around the world. His book *Celebrity Branding You®* has also been used as the textbook on personal branding for University students.

The CEO of The Dicks + Nanton Celebrity Branding Agency, an international agency with more than 1,000 clients in 26 countries, Nick is an award-winning director, producer and songwriter who has worked on everything from large scale events to television shows with the likes of Bill Cosby, President George H.W. Bush, Brian Tracy, Michael Gerber and many more.

Nick is recognized as one of the top thought-leaders in the business world and has co-authored 16 best-selling books alongside Brian Tracy, Jack Canfield (creator of the *Chicken Soup for the Soul* Series), Dan Kennedy, Robert Allen, Dr. Ivan Misner (Founder of BNI), Jay Conrad Levinson (Author of the *Guerilla Marketing* Series), Leigh Steinberg and many others, including the breakthrough hit *Celebrity Branding You!.®*

Nick has published books by Brian Tracy, Mari Smith, Jack Canfield, Dan Kennedy and many other celebrity experts, and Nick has led the marketing and PR campaigns that have driven more than 600 authors to Best-Seller status. Nick has been seen in *USA Today*, *Wall Street Journal*, *Newsweek*, *Inc.* magazine, *The New York Times*, *Entrepreneur®* magazine and, FastCompany.com, and has appeared on ABC, NBC, CBS, and FOX television affiliates around the country, as well as CNN, FOX News, CNBC, and MSNBC from coast to coast, speaking on subjects ranging from branding, marketing and law to American Idol.

Nick is a member of the Florida Bar, holds a JD from the University of Florida Levin College of Law, as well as a BSBA in Finance from the University of Florida's Warrington College of Business. Nick is a voting member of The National Academy of Recording Arts & Sciences (NARAS, Home to The GRAMMYs), a member of The National Academy of Television Arts & Sciences (Home to the Emmy Awards), co-founder of the National Academy of Best-Selling Authors, an 11-time Telly Award winner, and spends his spare time working with Young Life and Downtown Credo Orlando and rooting for the Florida Gators with his wife, Kristina, and their three children, Brock, Bowen and Addison.

CHAPTER 5

USE YOUR VOICE AND BODY LANGUAGE TO CREATE TRUST IN BUSINESS

BY TOM A. PUENTES AND JUAN CARLOS VAZQUEZ

Yes, we are about to give you the secrets on how to use your body language and voice to create trust in business. First, we need to make sure you understand that these principles will work as intended when you use them to achieve the ultimate goal: **to create trust for long lasting relationships in business.**

If you choose to build mutually beneficial relationships, based on **trust** (which we suggest is the proper mindset) we think you will find that what we have to say is powerful, practical and downright useful!

I have a story to share, but first let me introduce you to Donald Trump!

Let us imagine you have been given the opportunity to do business with Donald Trump, himself. Whatever your business with Mr. Trump may be, you will need all the help you can get. Of course, you have prepared like mad and have done all you know how to do to have your presentation sharp and ready. You are also aware (because I am about to tell you) of this very important piece of information from <u>The Definitive Book of Body Language by Alan Pease:</u>

Body language is an outward reflection of a person's emotional condition.

And in this same book, he gives us the following observations that cannot be ignored:

> "Our analysis of thousands of recorded sales interviews and negotiations during the 1970s and 1980s showed that, in business encounters, body language accounts for between 60 and 80% of the impact made around a negotiating table and that people form 60 to 80% of their initial opinion about a new person in less than four minutes."

Okay, so you really do *not* want to ruin your chances since your proposal is really good and the last thing you want to do is to act like a chump.

I will now give you a crash course on the effective body language you must use when creating trust in business. In this case, what you need to know before you walk into the beautiful and luxurious office of Mr. Donald Trump.

THE S.L.A.N.T. METHOD

This is where the S.L.A.N.T. method comes in. Before I begin, allow me to say that it would be wonderful to be able to talk about the language of clothes and how you should be dressed to go meet with Mr. Trump. However, for the purposes of this chapter I will assume that you are dressed "the part," otherwise, we know that you will be hearing the famous words "you're fired."

Imagine yourself there, in that glorious office. He is personally going to interview you, as this is obviously very important for him too.

The S.L.A.N.T. method is the quickest way to communicate confidence and create trust in business, let's understand why.

S.L.A.N.T.

S: STAND OR SIT STRAIGHT

The S signifies Standing or Sitting straight. When you stand or sit straight, you are consciously communicating to the other person he or she is important. If you can picture it in your mind, any time anyone is in front of a company president, a respected leader, or an honored figure of any type, the person is always standing "at attention." You must therefore stand straight and/or sit straight whenever you are facing Mr. Trump. This will immediately allow your own physiology to change, making you feel more confident and alert. This action tells Mr. Trump "This person is professional, and gives me the respect that I deserve." This is the first step in quickly creating trust.

You are about to sit down: make sure you UNBUTTON and open your suit jacket before you sit down.

L: LEANING TOWARDS THE PERSON YOU ARE TRYING TO CONNECT WITH

The L stands in this case, for you leaning towards Mr. Trump— regardless of whether you are in a standing or seated position. As you lean towards him, you always maintain eye contact. I will even tell you which eye is better to focus on: the right Eye.

Before today, you really did not know which eye to focus on when you speak to someone face-to-face in business. It's a great piece of information, since "The Donald" tends to be a very logical thinker, it will mean he is primarily using the left side of his brain. *Look at his right eye to activate the left side of his brain*. This will create a faster rapport with someone like him.

As you lean forward, whether standing or seated, you want to smile OPENLY. An open smile means that you show your teeth and the eyes are also engaged. Look at yourself in the mirror and practice a genuine open smile. As you do this, think of your favorite person, waving hello to you. Smile genuinely and pay attention at how your eyes immediately engage in the task without effort. If your eyes are not engaging, you are not showing a true open smile. Don't force it. Just practice until becomes natural.

Now, show both palms frequently. This palm up gesture is used as a sign of submission, openness and honesty. All of these gestures convey trust and are highly priced by anyone, especially Mr. Trump.

Continue to focus and imagine you are still in that glorious office. (Love the rich wood inside—don't you?)

While you lean, make sure both of your feet are pointing directly at him and that both soles of the feet are flat on the ground

A: ACTIVELY AND ATTENTIVELY LISTEN

There is a big difference between hearing someone and actively listening. Have you noticed that when you need a friend (a true friend) you sit next to him and he will literally "lend an ear"? Yes, picture how he will usually rotate his head and tilt it in order to have his ear towards you to hear you out, especially, if you are giving them all the juicy details of your story. It is a good idea then, to assume the same posture when Mr. Trump is speaking to you and asking questions. You actively listen and slightly turn your head to "lend an ear."

N: NOD WHEN IN AGREEMENT OR WHEN MAKING AN AFFIRMATIVE STATEMENT OR POINT.

The N stands for nodding. It is very important that nodding be done very carefully and authentically. If you are not being authentic, this could quickly change the mood in your meeting and make Mr. Trump believe you are a "Yes Man." Nodding can be compared to jewelry a woman wears. If done tastefully, it will greatly enhance any outfit that is appropriate for the occasion. If overdone or inappropriately used, it will ruin the outfit regardless of how expensive it may be. So how does this relate to nodding?

Nodding is a very powerful tool that should be used *when what you are hearing from the other person agrees with your personal values, core beliefs or deep thoughts on the subject*. Try not to nod more than three times in a row. It not only loses its effect, but it draws too much attention to it.

T: TRACK YOUR CLIENT FOR BODY LANGUAGE SIGNALS

Tracking is basically following a line of non-verbal action or thought.

You are looking at Mr. Trump to see if there are any other gestures or body language signals that you can use similarly to establish further rapport and therefore enhance trust.

As you become more experienced, and depending on the circumstances, it is important to keep an eye on two essential things while tracking Mr. Trump:

1. The speed and tone of the voice. If he is speaking slowly (if you see him slowly enunciate and mark his words) emulate the same pace and rhythm of talking. If he asks a question quickly, let your answer be at that same pace.

2. It is also important to match the speed and rhythm of his breathing. This creates a deep almost hypnotic effect that will facilitate trust. Mr. Trump will not know why he is starting to really like you.

Bonus Note: Should there be any objects between you and Mr. Trump, for example a glass of water or a cup of coffee, do your best to reposition the object so that is never between you and Mr. Trump. Just move it to one side or the other.

Alright: you are ready for your meeting with "The Donald."

Uh, oh, Mr. Trump just phoned. He can't have that meeting face to face, but he will talk to you on the phone!

Okay so you just wasted $3K on that Armani suit you bought only to shake his hand. I want you to focus your thoughts on how you are going to use *your voice* to create trust. I have spent the past 25 years primarily speaking with clients over the phone, building trust and long lasting relationships (which I am blessed to have).

In all those years I have learned you must pay attention not only to your words and language but also your speed, tone and delivery. Most important, you must learn to listen well, while being in the right state of mind. Your only goal is to establish a deeper relationship, building trust with the person, helping them without any hidden agenda.

The phone rings…

You are comfortably sitting at your desk looking dapper in that awesome suit (after all you decided to wear it while you talk to him, because it makes you feel ready and at the top of your game). You turn your computer monitor towards you and read to yourself the words "SLOW DOWN" which you wrote to remind yourself to pause and speak slowly. You take a deep breath and his secretary puts him on the phone… He greets you in a quick formal manner (typical of a busy tycoon), and he states he has read your proposal but tells you what he really wants to know is what's on your mind.

With a warm and nice greeting (avoiding the "Speedy Gonzalez" overly excited salesperson schpeel), you remind him of the highlights of your plan but as you finish, you tell him that you **feel** really interested in knowing how can you **fit his current needs**. Notice how his tone becomes more friendly and relaxed. You get him talking.

Now is your time to listen. Remember, he can't see you so instead of nodding as to affirm his statements and confirm that you are actively listening, interject an "I understand" or "I agree" when appropriate. The conversation goes on and he continues to talk. He tells you he is very inclined to accept most of your terms; he has had a "**great conversation**" with you. You are thrilled! You must have done something right and connected with Mr. Trump. You hang up the phone (after picking up your jaw from the floor in amazement of what just happened) and jot down some notes on how you have just used your voice to help you establish trust with Mr. Trump:

1. **SPEED.** You watched the speed of your voice and practiced pausing and slowing down.

2. **TONE.** You watched your tonality. Once he changed his tone of voice from formal and hurried to more friendly and relaxed, you did the same. You were aware of your voice delivery. **You let him set the pace**. You carefully listened to his breathing, speed and tone.

3. **LISTEN.** You actually let him talk. You realize that your pausing allowed for him to be more open towards you and got him talking. You conveyed humility. Phrases such as "I feel," "I understand" or "I agree" were interjected when sincerely meant.

4. **THE ACTUAL WORDS YOU USED.** You avoided the typical sales profile. You did not use phrases or words known to trigger negative feelings such as "I'm calling to follow up," "You need this, you need me, you need us" or "I'm calling to see if you are willing to explore the blah, blah, blah." Instead, you asked for more information, questions such as "Where do you think we should go from here?" "Does this make sense?" or "Would you be open to…" worked well. And yes, thankfully you refrained from asking him what he uses on his famous hair. Aaah…. All good.

But…what if he says NO?!

Since it's Mr. Trump we are talking about here, you are probably very disappointed and are thinking of banging your head against the wall but of course you want to save your brain cells for future use, therefore you will calmly say: "That's not a problem."

You practiced saying it out loud and noticed how it calmed you down and brought you a sense of peace. It also helps you not to get defensive and ruin your chances from ever working with Mr. Trump again.

Responding in this way helps reflects confidence in your service or product and that you would not sell it to anyone who does not fully appreciate it. Mr. Trump may even change his mind; after all he really liked you!

In any case, any time you get a no for an answer, think about it this way: The deal was not a good match for you; it was not a good fit for either of you. This is a positive outcome. Focus your efforts on creating trust with people whom you can help, and who in turn, will help your business grow as well.

In conclusion, your voice and your body language are truly fantastic tools and assets to help you build strong and successful relationships. Fine tune them and let them be tools for your business success. Use these principles to eliminate any bad habits that may reflect a lack of confidence or disbelief in yourself or what you sell or do.

It is our sincere wish that you go into all future meetings with your best foot forward. May you always do well in business and in life, and may your body and voice always speak "SUCCESS."

ABOUT TOM

Tom A. Puentes has been in the financial services industry since 1985. He is a Senior Vice President and Financial Advisor with Morgan Stanley Smith Barney, working in Seattle, WA, and Ventura, CA. His clients include family foundations, labor unions, health professionals, executives, Internet entrepreneurs, and business owners across the entire U.S. From 1989 to 2000, Tom hosted a weekly financial show called "Your Money Matters," on The Business Channel, station KWHY, Los Angeles. He was also the financial correspondent for KADY-TV in Ventura, CA.

Tom actively supports many local and national charitable organizations including Pacific Northwest Ballet and PNB School, Seattle Union Gospel Mission, Everett Gospel Mission, Good Cheer food bank in Langley, WA, Starlight Foundation, Beit Tikvah, American Red Cross (Board of Directors-Ventura CA), Seattle Symphony, Haitian Health Foundation, Hope to Haiti, Metropolitan Opera, Joseph Project, and Seattle Opera. Tom is committed to financially supporting philanthropic causes and has traveled in recent years to support such outreaches in Sri Lanka, Israel, and, most recently, Haiti.

Tom is an avid fan of the opera and attends as many operas as possible averaging 12-15 operas each year in New York, London, and Verona, as well as Seattle. He loves exploring new restaurants, taking in a Seattle Mariners baseball games, attending the ballet, symphony and jazz concerts, sailing, scuba diving, and exploring tropical beaches. Tom finds his greatest pleasure spending time with his grandchildren in the Seattle area and his wife Gretchen, with whom he has been love with since 1986.

Tom can be reached at tom.a.puentes@mssb.com or (360) 221-2021.

ABOUT JUAN

Juan Carlos Vazquez D.C.

- **Personally trained by the famous Speech and Image Consultant, Ms. Dorothy Sarnoff in Speech Dynamics, Body Language and Clothing Selection for Success.**

- **Personally trained in History of Lie Detection, Forensic Truth Verification, Computer Voice Stress Analysis, Advanced Kinesics (Body Language), and Interviewing and Interrogation by Dr. Charles Humble of the National Institute for Truth Verification.**

- **Completed the World Renowned program by Dr. Chester L. Karass on Effective Negotiating**

- **Honored member, National Directory of Who's Who in Executives and Professionals**

- **Past Qualified Medical Examiner for the State of California**

- **In 2005, named Man of the Year by the American Biographical Institute**

- **In 2008, the American Biographical Institute awarded Dr. Vazquez the Title of Outstanding Professional for Dedicated Achievements in the Field of Chiropractic Spinography**

- **In 2009, listed among Top 100 Health professionals by the International Biographical Center in Cambridge, England**

Dr. Vazquez has had the honor of co-authoring this chapter with his lifelong best friend, Mr. Tom Puentes. Dr. Vazquez has a passion for God, family and friends. He has been a practicing Doctor of Chiropractic for 22 years. His profession has taught him to observe body language for clinical purposes. He is married to his soul mate and love of his life, Mali. He has a wonderful daughter, Rachelle, who is attending a top University. Dr. Vazquez greatly enjoys spending time with his father, Tino, also his best friend and supporter. He would also like to thank his brother, Carlos Alberto Vazquez, a psychologist, for his unique insights into the human mind.

He can be reached at: nr5772@gmail.com.

CHAPTER 6

THE ULTIMATE MARKET OFFER –

THE MAFIA OFFER

BY "DR. LISA" LANG

WHAT IS A MAFIA OFFER?

A *Mafia Offer* sounds like something out of a movie, not something that could seriously help you make more money in your business by increasing and controlling your sales. When done correctly, it's a marketing miracle—a Mafia Offer is *"An offer so good that your customers can't refuse it and your competition can't or won't offer the same."* I will refer to the operational improvements required for a Mafia Offer as a competitive advantage.

A Mafia Offer is simply the offer you make to your market—your prospects and customers—to make them desire your products or services and something that your competition cannot quickly match. And, of course, the offer you make is a combination of your products, services, and how you deliver them. Moreover, for your offer—the solution you're selling—to be *unrefusable*, you are most likely offering something of equal or greater value than the price you are charging.

Many people confuse a Mafia Offer with a *unique selling proposition* (USP), *customer value proposition* (CVP), or a *sustainable competitive advantage* (SCA). USPs, CVPs, and SCAs take what you already do and state it succinctly and with more specificity aimed at one or a few of their customers' problems or gaps in current market offerings. These alternatives can be Mafia Offers, but most of the time they are not. Furthermore, a SCA is an operational or technological advantage and not an offer per se.

Most companies offer solutions that solve their customers' various problems or symptoms. With a Mafia Offer, we are addressing our customers' core problem as it relates to doing business with our industry.

A Mafia Offer typically requires that you do something different (make operational improvements to establish a competitive advantage) to address your prospect's core problem. These operational improvements allow you to actually deliver something unrefusable to your customers and something your competition can't (or won't) do because they are not willing to or don't know how to make the same improvements. In other words, you have to establish an operational advantage.

In this way, a Mafia Offer is a sustainable market offer built on this advantage. Mafia Offers are not a positioning or a tag line. They can only be created by satisfying a significant need of the market to the extent that no significant competitor can. A Mafia Offer is where we start if you have a market constraint.

DO YOU HAVE A MARKET CONSTRAINT?

Let's do a quick check. How would you answer this question? If I could increase your sales tomorrow by 20%, could you handle the increase while:

- being 100% on-time, to your very first commitment;

- without going into firefighting mode; and

- still maintain a competitive lead-time?

If the only way that you could handle the increase is to increase your lead-times, work overtime, or miss due dates, then you have an internal operational constraint. You don't have a market constraint. On the other hand, if you can answer yes and you could take a 20% increase in sales and not have any negative effects, then you likely have a market constraint.

DEVELOPING A MAFIA OFFER

To develop a Mafia Offer, there are three things that we need to consider.

1. **Your Capabilities: Both What They Are and What They Could Be, Compared to Your Competition.**

   Your capabilities are how you deliver your product or service. For example, what's your lead-time? Your due date performance? Your quality? Your answers to these questions are your capabilities. Typically, when we first start working with a company, their capabilities are similar to those of their competitors. If they were much better or much worse, they would know.

   From the figure of typical Theory of Constraints (TOC) results, if you were quoting a 6-week lead-time, we can expect a 70% reduction or a lead-time of less than 2 weeks after applying the TOC solutions to your operations. This gives us an idea of the competitive advantage that we can establish and capitalize on in our offer.

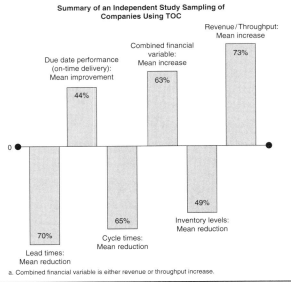

Summary of an Independent Study Sampling of Companies Using TOC

FIGURE 22-1 Typical results with Theory of Constraints. (Source: Mabin and Balderstone, 2000.)

2. Your Industry — How You and Your Competitors Sell Whatever You Sell.

The second thing we look at to develop your Mafia Offer is how your industry sells whatever it is that you sell.

The key is to understand how your industry interacts, in the selling and delivering of your products/services, with your typical prospects and customers.

3. Your Specific Customers and How They are Impacted by Typical Capabilities and How Your Industry Sells.

Since your customers are the only judge of your Mafia Offer, we also need to understand how your current capabilities and those of your competitors affect the companies in your target market, and how they are affected by the way you all sell to them.

It is in these interactions and interfaces that we may be causing negative effects for our customers and prospects. Understanding these negative effects leads us to uncover our customer's core problem relative to doing business with our industry.

The easiest way to understand what a Mafia Offer is, what makes it good, and how to create one is to go through an example. Most likely, this example won't apply to you because an offer is specific to a company and its particular customers. Nevertheless, you can gain by understanding how to apply the three considerations to a specific situation.

CUSTOM LABEL PRINTER—AN EXAMPLE

Let's consider a custom label printer. The labels this printer makes for one customer can't be sold to anyone else. However, the same customer may reorder a label for a number of years. Moreover, this label company's customers buy about 100 different labels for their various products. Many of their customers are regional-sized food and beverage companies. They produce food products in multiple flavors and put them in a variety of packaging, causing them to need 100 different labels.

The analysis started by evaluating the internal capabilities of this printer and those of their competitors. We found that this printer and their competitors generally quoted a 2-week lead-time. We also learned that the due date performance (DDP) was about 90% for this type of custom label printer.

To determine if this label company's performance was typical for their competitors as well, we simply talked to the salespeople. If a company's performance is much better or much worse than the competition, their salespeople will have heard about it. In this case, the salespeople indicated that the 2-week lead-time and the 90% DDP was neither praised nor a problem.

From our experience of working with printers in the past, we expected to get the time through the shop down to just a few days and to improve DDP to 99%. A quick tour through the shop verified that this should be possible. On the tour, we noticed a large amount of *work-in-progress* (WIP) and "ganging of jobs" to make the best use of setups.

With this information and knowing that the actual touch time of a job was measured in minutes, we were confident that the cycle time through the shop should go from the 2 weeks or more now to just a few days. We anticipated that we should be able to improve this shop to 99% DDP and the time it takes an order to flow through the shop should be dramatically reduced. Our estimate was two to three days.

Next, we turned our attention to the industry and how the industry sells custom labels. Now, if you've ever bought anything printed

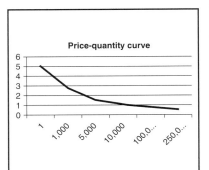

you know that the lower the price per piece that you want, then the more you will need to buy. If you only want one or a few pieces, then your price per piece will be very high. The printing industry uses a price-quantity curve like the one shown here.

In addition to a price-quantity curve, it was also standard practice to allow customers to spread the quantity across all their different labels. Therefore, if a customer needed 100 different labels they could spread the volume across all 100.

Next, we looked at the impact that the 2-week lead-time with 90% DDP along with the industry practices have on the label company's customers. In other words, what negative effects are we causing our customers because of our capabilities and how we sell?

In the case of this custom label printer, we selected a representative customer to understand the cause-and-effect relationship between how we sell and the impact it has on our customers. We selected a coffee roaster that purchased about 100 different labels and who, when they looked at that price-quantity curve, decided to purchase 6 months worth of labels at a time. Labels are relatively small and inexpensive, so holding 6 months of inventory was common.

To finalize the order of six months worth of labels, the coffee roaster needs to determine how to spread the quantity across the 100 labels. How many French Roast, Columbian Roast, and French Vanillas were going to sell in each size bag? To do that they had to forecast out 6 months how many of each label they

72

were going to need, which meant they had to guess:

- how much coffee all of us were going to buy;

- in what flavor; and

- in which size bag.

Now, if you only know one thing about a forecast, what do you know? That it's wrong! The only question is just how much is it wrong and in which direction.

Our practices force our customers to forecast. The forecast ends up being wrong in one direction or the other. If the forecast is low, their lines go down, causing them to lose productivity and to work overtime when they do finally get the labels in. Their costs also increase because, in addition to the overtime, they have to pay expedited shipping charges. And, the buyers are frantically working to get the labels in house and the line back up.

If the forecast is high, they end up with too much inventory of some labels. High inventory levels increase the likelihood of damage or obsolescence. High inventory results in higher carrying costs and cash tied up in unneeded inventory, and causes the company to hesitate before making any label changes.

Therefore, our analysis lead to the following Mafia Offer:

"Mr. Customer, don't give me orders. Your orders are based on your best guess of how many labels you think you might need. That's because label printers put that price-quantity curve in front of you and force you to have to guess out six months. The forecast ends up being wrong, and how can it possibly be right? Instead, tell us every day how many labels you use and we can guarantee, on the one hand, that you won't have to hold more than two weeks' worth of labels. And you know how your marketing department was complaining that they can't make the changes they want because you have six months worth of inventory? Well, now you will only have two weeks. At the same time, we will guarantee that we never stock you out. We will guarantee that you'll never go to the shelf and not have the label you need. And if we ever do stock you out, we will pay you $500 per day per label. We offer all this at the same competitive price you pay today and of course you will have a lot less of your cash tied up."

THE TEST — IS IT A MAFIA OFFER?

Let's test that offer against our definition. Is the offer so good our customers can't refuse it? Well, that depends on the customer. If we have done a good job with our analysis, it should be unrefusable to 80% of the target market. Realize that no offer will be 100% accepted by any market. There will just be some people, for whatever reason, that won't find your offer compelling.

When we develop a Mafia Offer, we start by asking to whom will the offer be made? We select a target market—a type of customer. The key is that our analysis is done with this target market in mind. In our example, most of the label company's customers were regional-sized food and beverage manufacturers. The offer was developed for those customers and prospects.

Equipment manufacturers also purchase labels. However, this offer would not work for them. They typically know that they are going to produce 100 machines this year and they know they will need 500 labels for those 100 machines. They do not have a forecasting problem to the same extent that food and beverage manufacturers do. They would not likely be moved by our offer, so our prospecting attention would be better spent on food and beverage manufacturers who struggle to keep the correct mix of label inventory while still having a mountain of inventory.

Therefore, we can conclude that this offer is unrefusable to our target market, but can our competition match it? We are asking our customers to hold 2 weeks' worth of inventory, down from about 6 months. What's the competition's lead-time? 2 weeks with 90% DDP. Therefore, there is no way our competitors could match the offer and not have to pay penalties or to hold a substantial amount of inventory at their risk.

As it turned out, we improved our flow from over 2 weeks to just 2 days (while sales and staffing remained constant), establishing the basis for a nice competitive advantage. Therefore, we should never have to pay a penalty as long as we are paying attention and we know how to react to the daily consumption data. So, this offer does meet the two requirements for a Mafia Offer. It is an offer the customer can't refuse and the competition can't offer the same.

Benefits to the Label Company

We previously discussed why the Mafia Offer was unrefusable for the label company customers. But what are the benefits for the label company?

- They stop the blah, blah, blah and sounding like their competitors. They can answer, "Why should I buy from you?"
- Sales increase (and so do profits if the TOC logistics solutions are used to improve operations).
- Time wasted producing labels that are not needed is eliminated.
- They gain 100 percent supply for label stock-keeping units (SKUs) included in the program.
- They substantially reduce the risk of losing a customer to a competitor over a small price reduction. Customers taking advantage of the Mafia Offer ask for long-term contracts.
- They became better at doing setups, and can easily run small batches, increasing their flexibility and responsiveness to the market.
- They became very good at adding new customers.
- Cash flow improves due to smaller batches and more frequent billing based on replenishment that is more frequent.

WHAT DID IT TAKE TO MAKE THE OFFER?

In addition to improving operations using the Theory of Constraints, the label company had to change their thinking in a number of areas. First, their offer would require that they do more setups. Ask any label printer how much it costs to do a setup and they will tell you to the penny. However, how much does it really cost?

Nothing! You don't pay your employees by the setup, and you don't pay your machine by the setup. The only real cost is a little paper and ink to get everything lined up. However, the label company's competition thinks that there is a real cost (due to allocations) and even if they could match the offer, they don't want to! They think the label company's costs will increase and they will go out of business.

The label company NOW understood that the true cost to do more setups was practically nothing and saving time on a non-constraint would save nothing. Setups do take more time, but an interesting thing happens when you start to do something more often—you get better at it! The label company freed up capacity by not wasting production time making labels that were not needed. So despite the additional setups, flow through the label company stayed at about 2 days.

So there you have it, an offer that is so good our customers can't refuse it and something the competition can't and won't match! The competition will not match this offer for some period of time and maybe never. Therefore, we've built and capitalized on a very sustainable competitive advantage.

Mafia Offers also work in service industries, project based industries, for non-profits and in many other situations. In addition to making a Mafia Offer to your customer you can also make a Mafia Offer to your vendors, your employees, your bank, your partners or affiliates, or for whomever you choose to target.

ABOUT DR. LISA

"Dr. Lisa" Lang is a renown Theory of Constraints expert and is the foremost expert in the world for applying TOC to marketing. Dr. Lisa is regularly sought out for her expertise on developing market offers that increase sales. She has been named a 2012 Trendsetter in *USA Today* for her work helping highly custom job shops and machine shops to become more productive, more competitive and to bring manufacturing back to the U.S. She has appeared in CNBC, CBS, *The Wall Street Journal*, and Yahoo! Finance to name a few.

As the President of Science of Business, she invented the Mafia Offer Boot Camp developing over 100 Mafia Offers for Fortune 100 companies, as well as, for small job shops. Dr. Lisa's *Mafia Offers: Dealing with a Market Constraint* book reached the #1 spot on the Amazon best-seller list. Dr. Lisa worked with Dr Goldratt, father of the Theory of Constraints, serving as the Global Marketing Director for Goldratt Consulting. During her tenure Goldratt Consulting was the fastest growing consulting company in the world. She has a PhD in Engineering and is a TOCICO certified expert. She is currently an officer on the TOCICO Board of Directors. Before becoming a consultant, Dr. Lisa worked for Clorox, Anheuser-Busch, and Coors Brewing.

Dr. Lisa is known for developing **"Mafia Offers" – offers so good that your customers can't refuse them and your competition can not or will not match them.** Mafia Offers are NOT unique selling propositions, value propositions or a competitive advantage. They are not price reductions or based on innovations.

To learn more about Mafia Offers and how you can create your offer in a 2.5 day Mafia Offer Boot Camp visit www.MafiaOffers.com and check out Dr. Lisa's bestselling book *Mafia Offers: Dealing with a Market Constraint*. Email Dr. Lisa at DrLisa@ScienceofBusiness.com.

www.MafiaOffers.com

CHAPTER 7

USING EFFECTIVE SALES CHOREOGRAPHY TO CREATE A WOW! CUSTOMER EXPERIENCE

BY SYDNEY BIDDLE BARROWS

When people ask me what I do and I tell them I'm a business consultant and my area of expertise is Sales Choreography and the Customer Experience, sometimes I get a few snickers. Usually from men, whose minds tend go directly into the gutter—oh, excuse me, bedroom. Yes, there certainly was bedroom action that went on in my former business, but it played a much more minor role than you might imagine.

"Bedroom action?!!? What kind of business were you in, lady?"

Well, I was in the Madam business, to put it bluntly. "Back in the day," I had a very elite escort service in New York City, and we catered to diplomats, international businessmen, Wall Street multimillionaires and Arab sheiks, as well as sports stars and musicians whose names you'd recognize immediately.

You can read the entire story in my first book, *Mayflower Madam*, which was a #1 *New York Times* Best Seller. It was translated into seven languages, reprinted 28 times in the U.S. alone, *Fortune Magazine* named it one of the Top Ten Best Business Books of the Year, and business schools across the country, including Harvard, used it in courses on Entrepreneurship, Starting Your Own Business, and the like.

Once that book hit #1, invitations started pouring in to give presentations to all kinds of groups (in particular, one extremely prestigious international business group that doesn't like to see their name in print, and I honor that request). After the presentation, titled "Marketing a High Cost Service" was over, I found the heads of these multi-million dollar companies asking me if I did "consulting." I had absolutely no idea what that was, so I blew them off, telling them I was "just too busy to do any consulting right now."

But after this happened a few times, I thought to myself, "Y' know, maybe I ought to find out more about this consulting thing, especially since it sounds like they'd pay me good money to do it." So I started to ask what they thought I might be able to help them with, and just listened.

> **STRATEGY #1** – Ask a lot of questions and then shut up and listen. Everyone's favorite subject is themselves or something that's important to them. Not only will people appreciate that you're genuinely interested in them, they'll tell you everything you need to know about what they want, why they want it, what hasn't worked in the past, and loads of other important information. And at the same time, they're talking *themselves* into why they need what you do, so all you have to do is encourage them to keep talking by occasionally asking leading questions and acting like this is the most fascinating conversation you've had all week. And it *should* be!

The terms Sales Choreography and the Customer Experience were completely unknown to me way back then. It had been *my* experience that the Client Experience, and the Sales Choreography that created and maintained it, was our <u>primary</u> business and the deliverables, the young ladies, were the <u>secondary</u> part of the business.

It turned out that these extremely successful businessmen caught on to this immediately, and wanted to engage my services because of the phenomenal success I'd had attracting clients, our consistently high conversion rates, the record-level of repeat business we did, and our ability to charge higher fees than anyone else, in spite of the fact that every one of our competitors was charging less, *and* we were also competing with free.

> **STRATEGY #2** – Is your primary business the Experience your Client has with you while purchasing The Thing, or is The Thing itself so unique that people can *only* get it from you? If you have competition that offers what appears to the untrained eye to be the same thing you offer, appealing and effective Sales Choreography is the only differentiating factor that will land you that customer and enable you to keep them. And if it produces an Experience that is unique, compelling, and really resonates with them, you can charge premium prices, too, which they'll gladly pay.

Remember, we choreographed the Experience from the second we landed on their radar screen, and this carefully crafted Experience continued throughout the entire sales process. It was meticulous Sales Choreography that:

➢ easily yielded a phenomenally high conversion rate (100% on many nights)

➢ consistently increased the original transaction size

➢ prompted them to call us far more frequently than they would have otherwise

➢ engendered tremendous loyalty – I'll never forget the night a client told me he'd "never demean (him)self by calling another agency"

➢ enabled us to charge higher fees than everyone else, in spite of the fact that all our competitors was charging less, *and* we were competing with free!

STRATEGY #3 – When you give your customers an Experience that resonates with them, you're giving more than just the product or service you're selling. You're giving them more value, and it's that value that motivates them to choose you, it's that value that influences them to return to you, and it's that value that inspires them to give you even more of their business. It's also that value they'll pay higher prices for: they feel they're getting more, so they're willing to pay more.

One of the first misapprehensions I'd like to dispel is that effective Sales Choreography has to cost money. There are instances where you do need to spend money, but only one of the unique and memorable Client Experiences we delivered cost the business an extra penny.

STRATEGY #4 – If funds are an issue, spend them on your best customers. It's more cost effective to spend money to keep them happy than to go out and look for new ones. That's how we did it, with very impressive results.

It could be successfully argued that I paid my phone girls more than the gum chewin' broads from Brooklyn who answered the phones at the other agencies, and that this cost "extra" money, but my phone girls were such a critical component of our Sales Choreography, that we couldn't possibly have been nearly as successful without them.

STRATEGY #5 – The people who are the first point of contact with your prospects and customers, and the sales people and customer service people who interact with them too, are *your most valuable assets.* If they're not first-rate, you'll have lower conversion rates, lower transaction sizes, less repeat business, and spotty referrals. It doesn't matter how terrific your product or service is if your prospects and customers aren't real thrilled with the way they're treated.

SOLUTION: pay those people good money and treat them like the gold they are, because if they genuinely like working for you, it will come across every time they interact with your customers. Happy employees are nicer, friendlier and more caring employees, more helpful employees, more loyal to the business, and more invested in its success. They'll stay with you longer, if not forever, and that continuity plays a major role in customer loyalty and retention, additional business, willingness to pay higher prices, and the level of referrals.

The most effective Sales Choreography involves nothing more than to make doing business with you inviting, inspiring, refreshing, fun – even something as simple as easy! Consumers today, more than ever, are looking for something different, something authentic, and something that *feels* good to them. They might not be able to articulate it, but what they're really looking for is a buying Experience that's:

1. Relevant to and resonates with them
2. Puts a smile on their face and in their hearts
3. Is interesting or enjoyable to take part in
4. Makes them feel really pleased, if not relieved, they've found you
5. Causes them to feel good about making the purchase, and
6. Makes them feel good about making the purchase from YOU

Not every business or every transaction will be able to incorporate all of these, but your customers need to experience at least four: particularly the last one.

STRATEGY #6 – Determine what kind of Experience your ideal customers are hoping to find and reverse engineer everything you do in order to create that reality. Design and integrate Sales Choreography that will engage and delight them, that will cause them to talk about you, and will influence them to look forward to returning.

There's no way of getting around it, persuasive and effective Sales Choreography does takes preparation and planning; you can't just wing it and expect to see results. There are several pieces that go into designing appropriate Sales Choreography, they're all interrelated, and each step has to be done in the correct order. Not knowing what the pieces are and the proper way to fit them together is why most people don't get it right.

Now before you can even think about designing Sales Choreography that delivers the desired Experience, you absolutely must have one thing very clear in your mind—actually, it should really be written down on paper. And that critical starting point is your story, or more accurately, your business' story.

The reason your business needs to have a story is because in order to create the appropriate Sales Choreography that's going to attract attention, stimulate interest and maintain that interest, you need a foundation to build it on, and the story of your business is that foundation.

The story of your business is made up of these three ingredients:

1. <u>The business you're really in</u>: What are the benefits, solutions, and outcomes your customers are hoping or expecting to get by owning your product or receiving your service? This is the business you are *really* in. Remember, these are very often not what they appear to be on the surface, but are all about reinforcing how they want to see themselves, be seen by others, or in some way fulfill other subconscious needs, wants or desires.

2. <u>Your USP (Unique Selling Proposition)</u>: This could be the unique nature of your product or service, the unique form in which it comes or the manner in which it's delivered, or it could be the uniqueness of the person or persons who are associated with it. It could also be the unique Experience prospects and clients receive before, during and/or after the purchase, or your USP could be *you*!

3. <u>The business your customers want you to be in</u>: This last ingredient is about the products and services you sell, *and* the manner in which you sell it and they buy it. It seems self evident to say you should offer a selection of products or services that's chosen specifically with the needs, wants and desires of your Ideal Customer in mind, but it's all too common for a business to offer a product or service because it reflects the owner's taste, he or she enjoys selling or providing it, or it's something they believe their customers *should* want. It's not enough to provide a particular product or service; you have to sell the appropriate *version* of it, the version *your* clients are looking for.

STRATEGY #8 – These are questions I ask every client at the beginning of every consulting engagement. How would you answer them?

1. What is it your customers are *really* paying you for?

2. What do they *really* hope or expect to get out of owning the product or receiving the service?

3. What *differentiates* your business from everyone else that does or sells what you do?

4. Why would someone choose to do business with you as opposed to your competitors?

5. What does your product or service offer that's *unique* only to you?

6. What are your best-selling products or services? Why?

7. Do you keep track of the questions prospects and clients ask about what you offer, particularly what it does or does not include?

8. Do you keep track of why people *don't* buy?

9. What do your closest competitors offer that you do not?

10. How does their Sales Choreography and the Experience that produces differ from yours?

If you attempt to design the most appropriate and relevant Sales Choreography for your Ideal Customers, so that they will have an Experience that really knocks their socks off *without knowing what the Story of your business is*:

➢ How are you going to position your product or service to appeal to your target market, what media will you use to reach them, and what will you say to get their attention and inspire a desire to find out more?

➢ How will you know which selling points to make, what benefits to emphasize?

➢ How will you know what information they need to hear or read that will make it more likely they'll book an appointment or make a purchase?

➢ How will you know exactly which words to use that will resonate with your prospects and trigger a desire to have what it is you're selling?

➢ How will you know precisely *which* products to carry or services to offer?

➢ There are so many ways to interact with people. Should you be doing that primarily over the internet, the phone, or in person?

➢ How do you manage that interaction? Do you want people to have easy access, make them "qualify" in some way, send them information first, make an appointment in order to get any more information, or simply stop by?

The Story of your business even governs the choices you should make regarding:

➢ the style of your website

➢ the location of your business

➢ the décor and ambience of your office or store

➢ the way you and your employees dress

In some cases, the Story of your business even makes a difference in the age, the sex, and the physical appearance of your employees.

If you follow these eight strategies, you'll have the information you need so that you, too, can create a level of Sales Choreography that will deliver the kind of Experience that will make your business stand head and shoulders above your competition, enable you to charge loyal customers premium prices, and build a strong, stable business that will more easily withstand any future economic turbulence.

ABOUT SYDNEY

Perhaps better known to millions as the "Mayflower Madam," Sydney Biddle Barrows found herself moonlighting as a phone girl at an escort service to supplement her unemployment check after having been fired for refusing to participate in a kickback scheme. It may have been the World's Oldest Profession but it certainly was not being run very professionally, and less than a year later she decided to open up her own agency. Relatively small but very upscale, Cachet prospered for five and a half years until New York's Finest closed it down, only to later publicly concede that it was the most honest and professionally run business of its kind ever operated in New York City.

Her first book, *Mayflower Madam*, went right to the top of the *New York Times* bestseller list; *Fortune Magazine* named it one of The Ten Best Business Books of the Year and business schools across the country, including Harvard, used it in their curriculum. Her fourth book, *Uncensored Sales Strategies*, co-authored with the legendary Dan Kennedy, was published in January of 2009.

Sydney Biddle Barrows is a recognized authority on using compelling Sales Choreography to create a meaningful and irresistible Customer Experience. She consults with entrepreneurs, businesspeople and professional practices to identify and analyze the Experiences their customers are currently encountering with them, their staff and their business in general. She then puts together a Sales Choreography Renovation Plan and works with her clients execute that plan.

Sydney also has an extensive speaking career and presents to a wide range of business groups, as well as guest lecturing at colleges and universities across the country, on *The Secrets to Creating a Unique and Compelling Customer Experience.*

In addition, she writes articles on the Customer Experience, puts out a newsletter called *The Experience Factor*, and contributes to entrepreneur.com (*Entrepreneur* magazine's online site) on the Customer Experience.

As an adjunct to her coaching and consulting business, Sydney does Roadblock Removal work, eradicating those roadblocks that sabotage people with the best intentions from organizing and using their time productively; from accomplishing the things they genuinely want to do; and that hold them back from being the kind of person they truly want to be.

Sydney lives in New York City on the Upper West Side, and has "no pets, no plants, no children, and no regrets."

Visit www.sydneybarrows.com for more information on her products and services, and www.roadblockremoval.com to find out more about how you can get out of your own way and live your life as the person you've always wanted to be.

www.sydneybarrows.com

CHAPTER 8

IT'S A MIRACLE!

BY DAVID WHITE

G etting into business, or growing your business, is so tough. I have been 'lucky' and hope to share with you how I had various shots at actually blowing myself up in the process. Everyone I have met has 'war stories' to tell! Most war stories are better to hear than actually live through.

I have put myself in harms way, I have become fearless. I have learned hard lessons.

I have learned from the best too, which includes Dan Kennedy. Probably like you I am nothing special, an ordinary chap born and brought up in the UK. My father was pretty good at his job and got promoted often, so I moved with the family north and south many times. I saw a lot of life, a lot of people, often stuck in their ways. Even now, I spend a quarter of my life—a week at least— in the U.S. and if not there, in Asia, South America or Finland. I'm not sure I totally recommend that, as it will not be agreeable to everyone. The more people I meet, the more stories I hear, the more I continue to learn. Continuous learning is a great interest, it keeps you on top and gives you opportunities to reach out to new and different people and ask for help. And generally, they do.

My story here is about interest and ambition. Growing up, I wanted to get into the electronics industry because I was interested in radios and TV, but also interested in fireworks and music. Then I started to become interested in young women. As I could not sing or play guitar (I had learned Tenor Horn) it meant I could not join a band. No one would have me. So that route to the women was, naturally, denied. I decided to make electronic instruments. I found the line "Would you like to play with my organ?" broke the ice. After a while I had to change to "Would you like to play with my bongos?"

I discovered at a young age that having the right story was important to getting what you wanted. Although I will not go into detail, the direct approach, (coming right out with what you wanted) was crass, and, as I quickly discovered worked a lot less, or not at all! Women are a fascinating subject, but not one we shall dwell on here.

To business. Unknowingly, I discovered one of the key secrets to sales. Storytelling. So, what better place to tell a story than in a chapter of a book? Although as you will discover, you can tell, retell and live through a story again and again anywhere. The neat thing about stories is they tend to be personal, about you, about human nature—and everybody has one. I discovered this was true in my electronics career too.

I was lucky enough to get the job I wanted and got paid to go to college as an apprentice to study electronics. This meant that in the summer months I had to actually go to work, which was a shock (until I discovered that work involved running down to the South Coast and installing / commissioning radar systems on war ships). I can tell you as a young man in your 20s, there is nothing better than working on big ships with missiles on board. That was where I rediscovered the power of Theatre.

As a young engineer, older folk, engineers and seamen would send me on missions for left-handed elbow grease and the like. Generally I did not have the gumption to say no, it was as much a game to them as me, although it had become tiresome. One day during commissioning, as usual, warning lights blinked red, and this time it was from up top. I was summoned to the deck. It could be cold outside so I put on my lab coat to keep warm, and anyway it made me look like a scientist. As I climbed to the top of ladder I could see across the deck a huddle of hot sweaty men in navel uniform and a small crane pulling out the munitions from one of the batteries. As I walked across, one particular missile was laid to rest on the deck and the men looked around to see me, a young boy with a tool box walking toward them. Of course I had seen this missile before many times, each was numbered and apart from that they were the real, heavy duty, fully armed, real thing. Live munitions.

I looked at the men, I looked behind me. I knew no one else was coming. They were hoping it was not this kid with his toy box and dentist outfit. Geeze, this missile could go off at any minute.

I nodded to the men and knelt down over the device. With speed and noise I unscrewed the panel and slammed it onto the deck. The men around me jumped. That was their first jump. Sensing their sensitivity, and wishing to make a meal of events I continued to clatter around, occasionally looking up. As I did I could see their anxiety. I saw beads of sweat roll down the side of more than one face. They clearly were not men used to dealing with live munitions, on a hot summer's day. The last thing they wanted was their lives in my hands.

I took out my pliers and hovered for a second over the blue wire. Talking to myself I muttered, "can't be" and looked up as I took my clipper off the blue wire and settled on the yellow. After a terrifying minute (for them) I tutted and looked up, saying "nope." By now, the guys had bulging eyes, red faces, and there were pools on the floor by their feet. They could not believe what was playing out. Was this thing going to blow?

Taking advantage I slammed my pliers down on the deck, I felt the men jump around me once more and I violently yanked a circuit board out of the missile innards and sent it spinning on the deck behind me. The men did not know whether to run, laugh or cry. I looked up once more and could see them saying their prayers. I deftly placed a replacement card inside, jammed it in by force and resealed the unit. Reran the test to Green and we were done.

Soon I was the sailors' hero, clearly the first 'Rocket Scientist' they had met. I had rediscovered theatre and found myself King of the hour. I got sent on a lot fewer errands after that.

I knew the same amount as when I was running errands, but now with a little staging, I found myself getting a lot more respect. Important lessons.

Years later I attended an X factor event in L.A. It was run by the Guru Jay Abraham. I heard his story on business transformation through optimization. Interesting. I met some very important people and heard some wonderful, emotional stories. Imagine 500 men crying with emotion hearing the founder of Fedex speak about how his company eventually made it. Rock Stars! It all made sense, but perhaps to bigger businesses, it did not seem like it was right for me (even though I was happy and full of emotional admiration for all I had met, and with all I had learned). I slept on it, and on coming home, in the plane, I had an epiphany. I realized I should set up Weboptimiser. Another lesson learned!

This was in 1996 at the beginning of the 'dot com' age. Since, Weboptimiser has become the World's most well-known Internet Marketing business. Weboptimiser outlived its competition and has traded for nearly 17 years, millions per year, delivering billions to clients. Our experience has ranged from helping IBM to Solo Practitioners with ideas and experience to share with all kinds of business owners and managers. From big names to one-man bands.

A few years ago, still connecting with Jay Abraham, I was introduced to Dan Kennedy. Dan one day explained that Jay certainly has all the theory, but he [Dan] puts it into practice—and Dan shares! Dan shares it in droves with thousands of business owners and managers small and large, through his newsletters, live events, mastermind groups and consulting. It was through Dan that I was invited to contribute to this book, because I am in his Titanium Mastermind Group. Through the power of story Dan shows how to communicate with a wider audience and he has taught me and my company, Weboptimiser how to share too.

Weboptimiser as a business focuses on delivering 'done for you' services and as a result, it is not appropriate to provide and share a lot of information on the specifics of the website, as we can talk more about *the opportunities* that the technology can lead you too, as I will cover later.

We created another business called Tribal Ideas which is a site we are continuously building, working on and adding to, where we reveal more about what we do in practice and we share there, too. At Tribal Ideas you too can learn about insider, real business developing tips and techniques you and your business can employ to get more out of Search and Social Media. We also include information on public speaking and presenting, as it is our objective to give you enough information for you to not just master the technology, but also to *master the management of the people that you will need to work with* whether they are colleagues or clients. It is our expectation you will get to such a size that DIY online marketing will be the furthest thing from your mind, at which time it would be useful for Weboptimiser to do it for you.

One important, vital observation I would like to share is that there is what I call Internet Speed and Human speed. My home broadband now operates at 20m /s, a tad faster than 16k dial up modem that I started with. Compared to that is human speed, which I believe to generally be considerably slower than even the slowest of slow 16k dial up. Gone are the times when you can just 'sell, sell, sell'. Nowadays, to sell, you need to cut through everyone else's promotions, communicate effectively, tell some deep routed stories and inspire. Your ideas have to become your customers idea. It becomes your job to make sure that you are the person to supply it. Let me attempt to provide an example on how Internet Marketing can be the glue to your sales campaign and how important story is to making the sale.

This example will not suit everyone's position, but as I learned from the Jay Abraham X factor event, unrelated ideas can lead to whole new businesses.

Many people know that they want to sell someone else's product. They do not have the resources to manufacture, design or invent, as most usually don't have the time or resources available. Most people usually need to earn an income efficiently and fast. So lets say you see an opportunity to sell some cream to dentists, a cream that helps reduce patient tension and fear. I choose dentists in this fictional example, only because everyone reading this should know what a dentist is. You know what a cream is right? All good so far.

Ok, although you know I am a 'rocket scientist' you should be starting to realize that this is not 'rocket science'. Reducing patient tension and fear could be of big importance to certain patients. But Dentists might not realize this is a problem, or could even be in denial. How do you solve this? The first thing to do is to let the dentists try it. Give them a sample and let them put a drop of the cream on the patients forehead to help create a calm and soothing environment. There are a couple of human psychological things going on here. The dentist will giving something to the patient and the patient will know that the dentist is not only thinking of the patient but doing something for the patient. So this is a very good procedure for the dentist. Afterwards the patient will in many cases be relieved that there was less pain and difficulty than expected and may like to buy some of the cream to take home. We have given the dentist something that makes him look good and provided an income stream.

There are several problems we want to overcome to make this a success. 1) Getting it to the dentist in the first place, with cost and time issues. 2) Making the sale. 3) Ensuring that sales occur again and again so that volume rises. 4) Locking out the competition.

Two scenarios present themselves, for the first imagine that what you have becomes a well known brand, what name would you use (working backwards)? You could choose Best Dentist, or Happy Patient. Both domain names are unused and for sale! Now when you market the product you have a name that is related to one of the key benefits, you could market both names, but that's another story. The Best Dentist is known by Happy Patients could become the strap line. In this way you are making both the sales pitch and potentially locking out the competition. In this case, as you established the name, pay per click will be low cost and SEO and Social Media Marketing both easy opportunities.

The second scenario is a new product with its new name, you need to get it into the hands of dentists. You have the option of sending samples to doctors, to patients and outright sale. You could visit householders or dentists, an expensive and difficult option when the world is such a big place. You will probably find that Direct Mail is best used when targeting Dentists and what better way than to put product in their hands then to post it to them. You could try telephoning them first (skype makes every call a local call) and then recording their level of interest in a database. Immediately following a call with a sample would work well and, knowing the names of the individual you could send them a personalized URL such as david.white.bestdentist.com where you could offer a sales letter providing the opportunity to log in or set up a personalized private account. There you could offer stock for sale and show videos of happy patients and their best dentist.

This scenario, albeit simplified shows how online can be integrated with offline marketing and real world people. Go visit TribalIdeas.com and set up your free account where I can show and share more. You'll find its not rocket science. TribalIdeas.com

ABOUT DAVID

My first technology venture was the founding of Saga Systems in 1981. Based in London, I started off as an engineer in Missile Guidance, so you could refer to me as a *bona fide* Rocket Scientist. While there I designed a keyboard to work on home computers and went on to earn my first millions at a young age (Saga Systems). I drove a Porsche, bought a house, got married and had a son.

All good? Not so much.

Just a couple of years later computers updated, I could not sell any more keyboards, I had lost my house, smashed up my car and was divorced. I was also penniless and my former wife was not allowing access to my new-born son.

My life had been reset.

I had lost everything in life that I had ever cherished. I struggled to make ends meet with less than £1000 to my name. No job, no business, everything lost and with maintenance (alimony) to pay, I was in trouble. I had no alternative but to take shelter at my parents' house and there I had to suffer my mother hounding me out of bed every day to go to work, to go to find work, to do something. Of course, I thank her now, but at the time, it was unbearable.

From here the only way was up! I WAS getting things done. I got a job at KFC and I sold sandwiches at the industrial park. I tried to get a real job in the afternoons. I was soon selling computer networks in those same industrial parks. There was more money in that!

Nevertheless, it was a tough life. Something HAD to change.

I was still basically broke, but I had something; I received an invitation to attend an event in Los Angeles. It was a MAD thing to do but I cashed everything and paid for the flight. Ienjoyed the Californian sunshine and the company, I heard inspiring stories, and I set about changing my life. On the plane home I determined, back in 1996, to set up and register Weboptimiser.com.

****

David served as the Chairman of the Search Task Force for the Internet Advertising Bureau for over two years. During that time, his best-practice standards were adopted by all good providers in the Search Engine Marketing industry. He is still chair and speaks at industry events around the world.

In 2010 he was a guest, as the Online Marketing Expert, on "The Brian Tracy Show", which was aired in the US. The program featured on NBC and was syndicated out to many other channels. He has also appeared on Sky News and LBC radio.

The appearance on the "The Brian Tracy Show" was partly the result of co-authoring "The Relationship Age" in which "The world's leading experts teach you PROVEN strategies for creating profitable relationships in the world of Social Media" along with Mari Smith, who is known as the pied piper of Social Media, and others.

"The Relationship Age" quickly became an Amazon Best Seller, and, due to the book's success, David was awarded a Best-Sellers Quill Award by the National Academy of Best-Selling Authors in New York in December 2010.

More recently, David co-authored "The New Masters of Online Marketing: Leading experts from around the world reveal proven secrets to grow your business through OnlineMarketing Strategies". That too became an Amazon best seller.

He has been behind the scenes, kept busy developing campaigns for major retailers and hotel groups across the World, working most notably with Ford, Marriot and most recently Virgin Money. He works with major brands to 'one man bands'. As David says, "It's not the size that's important; it's the challenge."

Today he continues to work on client accounts. He has become increasingly involved in the world of Social Media, particularly with the development of iMA profiling systems and video. His experience has grown from search to all aspects of traffic generation to lead-capture techniques, membership sites, video and mobile optimisation to real world business development for client companies.

He is a fully-fledged and paid up member of Dan Kennedys 'herd' and is currently part of the Titanium Mastermind Group.

You can learn more about David's business at Weboptimiser.com by clicking on "site audit" on the site's top menu where you will find a free offer for him to analyse your web site and get back to you with optimisation ideas; ways that you can make your business work better on and off line.

CHAPTER 9

4 KEYS TO A SUCCESSFUL SOCIAL MEDIA OPTIMIZATION PLAN

BY TOM BUKACEK

I remember how frustrated I felt on that hot August afternoon, driving 30 miles from my house to meet a potential home buyer in Manor, Texas, only to have the him stand me up. I still remember how much I hated waking up at 3am every Saturday to travel throughout Austin, Texas, so I could hammer in my *'We Buy Houses'* bandit signs into the dry, hard ground in order to try to attract home sellers. I also recall what it was like placing my *'We Buy Houses'* business cards on car windows in parking lots, getting dirty looks from customers and being chased off by business owners who wanted me out of their parking lot.

There had to be better ways of generating leads, right?

Sure, direct mail got me the occasional lead. I was printing out and sending 50 handwritten yellow letters every day to houses on the pre-foreclosure list. I was advertising in the Greensheet and had an ad in the Yellow Pages. I was doing all the traditional marketing stuff I was taught in every marketing class I'd ever taken.

Unfortunately, so were a couple thousand other real estate professionals in Austin. The traditional methods of advertising were very costly and were also not very effective.

But what really frustrated me the most in the summer of 2010 was how my friends, Curt Maly and Nick Bridges, who were also real estate investors, seemed to be able to attract leads without all the hassle. What marketing miracle had they uncovered?

How did they transform their real estate business from hours of mind numbing labor to getting their phone to ring without leaving their house?

Fed up with high marketing costs and low results, I was open for a new idea. I decided to call them and take them out to lunch so I could find the answer.

INTELLIGENT ONLINE MARKETING SYSTEM

Curt and Nick were able to relate with my frustration as they had dealt with the same challenges I had. However, things had changed for them. They were able to find as many leads as they needed without having to leave their houses.

They had created an intelligent online marketing system that produced leads for them 24 hours a day, 7 days a week, regardless of if they were awake or sleeping; in town or on vacation.

The only part of their system that was missing was a writer, and given my love and experience for writing, a new partnership was formed. It was at this moment that I began my journey on discovering the power of Social Media Optimization.

FIRST CUSTOMER

I wasn't the only one who had noticed that Curt and Nick were having success online. A local real estate guru named Phill Grove also wanted assistance bringing in customers. Phill was getting ready to launch his new real estate education product and wanted our assistance in promoting his brand online. We implemented our social media optimization processes for him and we were able to surpass his goals.

A month later, Internet marketing guru Mike Dillard was releasing his new product and invited us, along with 100 other Internet marketers, to sell his products. Unlike the competition we were facing, we had no mailing list to pitch. We were starting this competition from scratch, in need of a miracle if we were going to have any success. Rather than focus on what we didn't have, we simply implemented our social media optimization process that we had used to attract customers in real estate.

At the end of the contest, we were one of the top earners. This accomplishment was exciting for us because it meant that what we were doing worked for industries other than real estate. In fact, when Mike Dillard heard that we had promoted his launch promoting only through social media, he wanted to meet us to find out exactly what we were doing.

We had coffee with Mike and explained our social media optimization process. While a genius at traditional and Internet marketing, Mike hadn't yet dipped into social media. He was blown away by what we had shared with him.

"*Look*," said Mike. "*If you don't form a company and apply what you do for others, then I will and I'm going to become rich doing it instead of you.*"

When a guy who just made millions tells you that, it's time to get serious about creating a company.

Shortly thereafter, Curt, Nick, and I shut down our real estate businesses forever and created Black Box Social Media, a company that was dedicated to utilizing Web 2.0 marketing techniques to help people of all industries brand themselves online.

Now Black Box Social Media provides services to many different types of clients including Physicians, Best-Selling Authors, Motivational Speakers, Reality TV Stars, Professional Sports Teams and more.

Regardless of who we work for, our social media optimization processes pretty much stay the same.

So what is our secret? What strategies did we develop and what processes did we create that had multimillionaires seeking us out for our services?

Here are the 4 keys that we use in every social optimization plan we create for our clients.

THE 4 KEYS TO A SUCCESSFUL SOCIAL MEDIA OPTIMIZATION PLAN

KEY 1: SOCIAL NETWORKING SITES

When most people who aren't familiar with the power of social media marketing think about using Facebook and Twitter, they imagine their kids using it to post funny pictures or send out irrelevant messages to their friends. However, social media optimization is not your 16 years old's Facebook!

There is an actual science for using Facebook, Twitter, Google+, Pinterest, YouTube and other sites for branding yourself and your business. The best form of marketing has always been word-of-mouth marketing, and when you think of it, social media is simply word of mouth marketing that happens online.

People are in the habit of visiting social networking sites every day, however, they're not going to be in the habit of visiting your specific Facebook site unless you are interesting and provide a reward for doing so. Here are three very important keys to having success on social networking sites:

1. **Post pictures of your product in action**. People love looking at pictures. It's a fantastic way to demonstrate the experience that your product or service offers. If you have a business where customers come in to interact, then take pictures of them in action. For example, if you have a restaurant and a group of people come in to celebrate a birthday, take photos of the group, let them know that it will be on your Facebook Page, and give them a card with instructions encouraging them to 'Like' your Page and how to share these photos. This little tip will allow you to quickly increase the number of 'Likes' on your Facebook Page. In this scenario, posting these photos

provides social proof that your establishment is a fun place to come into and celebrate birthdays and other events. Plus, the average Facebook user has 214 friends, so if they 'share' your photo on their site, you will have more people becoming aware of your business and seeing exactly how much fun they can have there.

2. **Run contests**. As the old axiom goes, *'you get what you reward,'* so if you want to have people continuously visiting your social site, posting, commenting, and overall engaging, then you should create contests that will reward this behavior and create a habit. There is software available that will track engagements among multiple social media sites, like Facebook, Twitter, and YouTube. Create a fun prize and you'd be surprised how many people will be incredibly motivated to promote your site to their friends.

3. **Engage with others**. Always acknowledge or respond to people who post on your site. People love recognition, and a 'Like' or comment or response to their engagement is a reward. Rewarding people on your site will condition them to come back to your site and participate again.

Once you've followed the above steps to incentivize your visitors to habitually check your Page, you can then use the site to subtly promote your product, services, or upcoming events. The Facebook Timeline Page for Brands and Twitter Brand Pages both allow you a banner for advertising that visitors will see each time they visit your site. For example, one of my clients is a Realtor. Every time she sells a house to a new couple, she takes a photo of them smiling with their house in the background and her Realty sign in the front. She then formats the photo to match the dimensions of the Facebook Timeline Cover Page requirements and sends it to new homeowners as a gift. The new homeowners love the photo and use it as their cover, which allows them to advertise not only their new house, but also the agent's information as well.

There are many other creative ways to use social sites to promote your brand. When seeking ideas, don't just limit yourself to text; include pictures and videos as well.

KEY 2: VIDEO MARKETING

If a picture is worth a thousand words, then a video is worth a million.

Video marketing is the biggest trend in online marketing because it's a great way to deliver your unique message in a seemingly personal manner.

People are tired of nameless and faceless companies and want to see the man behind the curtain. Video allows you to deliver a personal message, demonstrate how to use a product or how a service works, answer questions, and make people more comfortable with their buying decisions. They're also the best medium for testimonials!

I unknowingly fell for the power of video marketing when searching for a Chiropractor after a car accident a couple of years ago. I'd searched online had visited a few sites, but the one that grabbed me was the one with a personal message. The Doctor had created a welcome video where he discussed his history, introduced his staff, and took you on a virtual tour of the office. By the time I arrived at the clinic for the first time, I already knew everyone who worked there, had seen the waiting room, knew exactly what to expect on the first visit and had already made the decision to become a patient. You cannot accomplish this type of personalized marketing through any other type of medium.

KEY 3: PAY PER CLICK MARKETING

Social networking sites, like Facebook, will reward you for receiving engagements and punish you posting low quality messages by not having your posts show up as frequently. On average, only about 17% of your fans will see your message. This statistic means that if you have 1,000 fans, only 170 people are seeing your message and 830 people who were interested enough to 'Like' your page no longer hear from you. So how do you reach the other 83% who aren't seeing your updates in their newsfeeds?

Many people familiar with pay per click marketing on social networking sites will tell you that it is a great way to drive new traffic to your social media pages, but did you know that pay per click (PPC) offers a tremendous, cost effective way to also reengage those 83% who have fallen off the radar?

With PPC marketing, you can target very specific online demographics of your potential customers by zip code, sex, age, marital status, interests, education level, and even place of employment. With Facebook PPC, you can even target those who are currently fans or not fans of your Page.

The simplest form of Facebook PPC marketing is to promote an ad from a Page post. This strategy will allow you to promote a specific post that will show the picture associated with the post and highlight the first couple of sentences of the message. Your fans will see this ad on the right hand side of their Page, click it, and become reengaged with you once again. Even if they don't click on it, they will still see your message and have a reason to reengage with your Page again. These types of campaigns can be run for as little as $15 for a day and still have a tremendous effect. If this type of service seems intimidating, don't stress as PPC management can easily be outsourced to other companies.

KEY 4: LOCAL ONLINE SEARCH.

I have a client who is a doctor that ranks on page 1 of Google whenever anyone in her city searches for a dentist. What's remarkable about this feat is that she doesn't even have a website. In fact, she's yet to pay a single penny and she is still able to rank on page 1 of Google and has her phone ringing off the hook with customers. How is this possible?

She has her business listed on all of the relevant local online search directories.

Over 90% of people go online to look for specific businesses close to them, yet surprisingly, only about one third of all businesses are listed online. Isn't the whole idea of marketing to be located in places where your potential customers are looking?

Those companies, like my dentist client list above, who are listed, optimized, and consistently updating their information on multiple local online search directories will put themselves in a great position to be found by potential customers seeking their services. Sites like Yelp, Manta, Google+ Local, Yahoo! Local Business, Bing Business Portal, and AOL Yellow Pages will show on page 1 of the search engine rankings when people search for a business. And most of these sites won't cost you anything!

Therefore, if you are a restaurant, a professional of any type, or have a local business, it is an absolute must that you become listed in the above business directories or else you run the risk your customers finding your competition instead.

One final tip: in addition to listing herself in multiple directories, she also encourages reviews and comments on these sites. The most interaction you have on local search directories, the higher up the search engine rankings your business will climb.

SUMMARY

In conclusion, our company has had a great deal of success following the same type of steps for ourselves and our clients. By creating multiple social networking sites, using photos, utilizing videos for marketing, creating pay per click campaigns, and getting listed on multiple local online search directories, we have been able to drive traffic to our own and our customers' websites. The great news is that the social optimization tips described above is no miracle; it is simply a process that anyone with the right knowledge can replicate and have the same success as us.

ABOUT TOM

Unlocking the 'Black Box' secrets of online marketing

Tom Bukacek is an author and social media marketing expert sought out by professionals seeking to brand themselves online. Tom utilizes the latest web 2.0 marketing strategies, such as social networking sites, video marketing, local online search, pay per click, article marketing, web design, and more. His clients include real estate professionals, doctors, bestselling authors, motivational speakers, Reality TV stars, professional sports teams, and more.

Tom recently spoke at the NBA owners meetings in Chicago about how they can improve their online presence.

Along with business partners Curt Maly and Nick Bridges, Tom is the owner of Black Box Social Media and co-creator of 'Social Media In 7 Minutes', an online training and implementation program designed for small businesses to learn how to utilize Facebook, Google+, Twitter, YouTube, and other social media sites for marketing.

This highly acclaimed program will show anyone how to create and implement their own online marketing plan without having to spend hours researching by utilizing their video training programs. In addition, Social Media In 7 Minutes also provides users with their very own all-in-one social dashboard, which will allow you to post on all of your social sites from one location in less than 7 minutes a day.

For more information on Tom, his company, his services, and to receive a free copy of his ebook 'Social Media Domination', please visit www.BlackBoxSocialMedia.com or call (512) 501-6414.

CHAPTER 10

YOU DON'T NEED A MARKETING MIRACLE:

PREDICT SUCCESS WITH YOUR SALES

BY RICHARD SEPPALA

E veryone's looking for a marketing miracle. That's why this book has that title—it's guaranteed to bring in readers.

And to be sure, there are a lot of great business experts in this book who will give you a lot of awesome ways to achieve marketing miracles. But you know what the dictionary definition of a miracle is?

"An extraordinary event. A wonder. A marvel."

What does that indicate? That miracles are extremely rare—and awfully hard to come by. Wise men (and women, for that matter!) have sat around expecting miracles for thousands of years, only to be disappointed.

Today, businesses continue to wish and pray for marketing miracles. They might begin an online campaign or send out a direct mail offer they desperately *hope* will reach the right people with the right message.

But, if it's based on strictly on guesswork and hunches, they're not likely to experience that miracle.

They're more likely to lose money on those campaigns.

Don't get me wrong, you may be the lucky one to make a marketing miracle happen. As for me, I don't want my clients to have to wait for a miracle. I'd rather see them make money *now*.

That's why I help my clients create marketing systems based on a predictive approach that helps them buck the odds and achieve profitable results. And I'll let you in on the secrets behind that approach in this chapter.

MY "ROI GUY" MISSION

In my guise as "The ROI Guy," I'm not exactly a superhero like Spider-Man, Batman or Iron Man. I can't fly through the air or zap super villains. I don't drive an indestructible slick car with special weapons hidden in the bumpers. No, I drive a Nissan (which *does* get pretty good mileage...).

What I can do—and what I've devoted my professional life to—is radically improve my clients' bottom line.

As I always tell people, I left the big corporate world to help the small guy. I learned all the high-level marketing strategies that the big boys employ—and I worked on ways to make them easy and affordable for small and medium-sized businesses that otherwise would never be able to benefit from them.

The biggest thing that multinational corporations can do that smaller companies can't is tracking and research. You think Coca-Cola or McDonalds goes out there with a giant campaign that costs millions and millions of dollars expecting a marketing miracle? I don't think their stockholders would exactly embrace that approach.

No, those kinds of major players put millions into researching their markets and generating numbers so *they know exactly what to expect* when they actually pull the trigger on an advertising effort.

So, if you have a dental practice, a legal practice or even an online or brick-and-mortar store, why can't you do the same?

Well, that's a miracle that is achievable—if you put the right systems to work for you.

THE SECRET TO BUSINESS GROWTH

There's only one way to grow a business, no matter what kind of business it is. And that's to get new customers or clients in the door. You can only up sell your current customer base to a certain extent, and you'll always have retention problems no matter how good your operation happens to be. People move and people change to another provider for various reasons.

The cold hard fact is that the pool of people who at this moment pay you for your products and services will only shrink—which is why it's essential to find reliable and consistent ways to find new customers.

Unfortunately, it's incredibly expensive, using conventional methods, to actually *get* those new customers. It's the most costly kind of marketing there is—six to seven times more costly than marketing to your current customers, according to Frederick F. Reichheld of the Bain Company. Most businesses end up taking an old-school "Spray and Pray" approach (selling to everyone in an attempt to attract a couple new big spenders). It's a huge waste, but most businesses don't see another choice.

That's because there's no way around this harsh fact of reality. *You need new customers*.

And ideally, those new customers would be like your best current customers. You know, the people who spend the most with you without blinking an eye; the 20% of your customers who generate 80% of your revenues. You want more like that 20%.

Well, believe it or not, that current 20% can actually help you get a whole lot more just like them—and boost your revenues like nobody's business.

Except we're not talking about nobody's business improving their bottom line. We're talking about *your* business.

DIGGING INTO YOUR DATABASE

"Your database is a goldmine."

How many times have you heard that old marketing stand-by, only to be left with the feeling that it was more bull than bullion?

If you're like most businesses today, you use your customer database to market to your list of past and present customers. You might be offering additional products or services, upselling them on current ones or trying to get them back in to buy if they've been away for while.

But, as I mentioned, that list can only take you so far in terms of improving your profit picture. Rather than being a goldmine, that database is more of a bedrock—providing the foundation of your current business. You obviously have to make sure that foundation has to stay solid. But you also obviously must have a plan in place to continue to grow your business beyond them or you won't have a viable future.

Beyond your database, who do you market to? How do you know where to spend your marketing dollars so that you reach the customers *most likely to buy from you?* Anyone else is, to be honest, a waste of advertising dollars.

Unfortunately, that waste is the norm for most businesses. They don't know who to market to, so, instead they target everyone that happens to be on a generic marketing list that's grouped by income or zip code or some other arbitrary criteria—even though 99.9% of those people will not become a new customer (let alone a *lucrative* new customer).

There is another way, though. Because, it turns out, your database *is* a goldmine. You just have to know how to mine that gold.

DISCOVERING "DATABASE DNA"

For years, I've been creating marketing tracking systems for my clients, culminating in the creation of my "ROI Matrix." The ROI Matrix took the marketing tracking process to a whole new level. It's able to compute, down to the penny, how much in profit each of my clients' marketing campaigns generated. It also features automated follow-up marketing and lead contact information collection. This made it incredibly easy for my clients who don't have the time or staff to do these kinds of vital marketing functions.

With The ROI Matrix, a business was able to see which campaigns were most effective, so they could focus on those messages and campaigns. Big problem solved. But there was still one big problem *un*solved that continued to bug me —and that was what I just talked about. The right marketing system could show you what the best message was, what the best way to deliver that message was...but it still couldn't reveal *who* were the best people to deliver that message to.

I was driving around in my car one day, thinking about all this, when I realized the answer to this dilemma. It was pretty simple, really.

I wanted to find the best possible new customers for my clients. Well... shouldn't we look at their *current* best customers and see what they had in common? For example, were they married or single? Did they have kids? How heavily did they use their credit cards? What levels of discretionary spending did they do? What was their average age range?

Now, once we correlated all that data, shouldn't we be able to then target *other* new leads that share those traits?

The question was, would this actually predict who would be the next generation of "best customers" for a business? Could we convert these leads to create a new wave of growth and revenue?

Fortunately, I had the perfect "test market" to try this theory out on.

PUTTING IT INTO PRACTICE

Not many marketing experts have the advantage I have: a spouse who's a successful dentist and also willing to let me use her practice as my marketing lab. I've been able to perfect many new and innovative techniques thanks to her (and she's a pretty good wife too, by the way!).

It was the perfect place to try out Database DNA. The first step was obvious—we had to determine who her best customers were. Once we did that, I put my "ROI Guy" expertise to work on their data. We have over 61 million email addresses in our database that we can extract demographics from which meant we could examine in detail the "DNA" of my wife's best customers and create a profile that contained the traits they had in common.

And by the way, if you think you already *know* what kind of people your best customers are, you might want to wait until you actually know what *your* specific Database DNA is. In my wife's case, I asked her to guess what her best customers were like in all the important categories. She made what she thought was a good appraisal.

Then I sprung the real facts on her—and she was shocked to find she was completely wrong; her best customers were actually the *opposite* from what she thought! It was another case of demonstrating to me that, if you market on the basis of assumptions, you may be completely off-track—and also another rock-solid validation of the necessity of digging into the Database DNA of a business.

We took this composite profile of her best customers and then cross-referenced it against the profiles of many non-customer leads to see who matched up—and, in the process, we found *thousands of other people out there who were strikingly similar to that "best customer" profile.*

Once we created this list of potential "best customer" leads, we then uncovered their physical street addresses, so we could target them with a special direct mail campaign from my wife's dental practice. We split that campaign into three different categories, depending on the specific demographics involved: Empty Nesters (older couples whose kids had grown up and moved out), Married Couples who were successful but didn't have children, and Very Successful Families, where the couple had kids and were doing well financially.

This was really exciting because, according to our figures, we were targeting people who spend *120 times more than the average customer.* That's a pretty good basis for a marketing campaign, wouldn't you think? Not only that, but through Database DNA, we were also eliminating 90% of the traditional marketing list, creating the ultimate "waste management" when it comes to the cost of a campaign.

The more I thought about it, the cooler it seemed to be. Just as The ROI Matrix tracking system had eliminated the cost of marketing campaigns that don't work, now my Database DNA system could eliminate the cost of marketing to leads that don't buy.

So we went ahead and implemented that direct mail campaign to our special targeted "best customer" profile list. And the results were astounding. Traditional response rates for dental direct mailings were anywhere from .05 to 2%, 2% being outstanding. These were considered to be *successful* results.

Well, the response rate on our "best customer" profile list was over three times that top number—an awesome 7%!

And I didn't even mention another great bonus of this process. Because my ROI Guy crew had already done their demographic due diligence on these leads, we already had the access to critical information about them. That meant, when someone would call my wife's dental office in response to the direct mailing, we would instantly be able to dig further into their "Database DNA" to determine just how much in dental products and services they would qualify to buy.

THE ONGOING VALUE

Finding a lucrative potential lead is like finding a needle in a haystack, or so most businesses think. So they market to the entire haystack, hoping they'll come across that sought-after needle along the way (which is why response rates do commonly come as low as below 1%).

The Database DNA system is designed to find those needles in advance—only to me, they're not just needles. I like to call them "Diamond-Encrusted Needles," because they're so rich in possibilities.

As more and more information becomes available on leads thanks to advances in technology, it's silly not to uncover and leverage that data to your advantage—especially when it can be used in such an affordable and effective way. That's why I put my ROI brain to work on how to identify the best possible leads from that data and why I was so pleased with the results.

There's no question that "one-size-fits-all" marketing is just a waste of time and money for most of us. Let Coke and McDonalds do the huge multi-million dollar image ads—small and medium-sized businesses don't have that kind of marketing budget to throw around. Nor should they have to.

When you target the top-paying customers with this kind of precision, you're engaging in granular marketing on a whole new level. There may be only one person on a particular street in your area that might be the right person to sell your products and services to. With Database DNA, we can find that person for you.

And that, to me, sounds like a real Marketing Miracle!

ABOUT RICHARD

Richard Seppala, also known as "The ROI Guy™," is a marketing expert, business consultant and best-selling author who helps companies maximize their profits by accurately measuring the ROI (Return on Investment) of their marketing efforts. His latest revolutionary tracking system, "The ROI Matrix," measures to the penny just how much revenue each specific marketing placement generates for a client.

Richard founded his "ROI Guy" company in 2005. In addition to his acclaimed marketing tracking systems, called "The Holy Grail of Marketing," he also supplies businesses and medical practices with cutting-edge sales solutions designed to facilitate the conversion of generated leads to cash-paying customers.

By identifying marketing strengths and weakness, The ROI Guy™ is able to substantially boost his clients' bottom lines by eliminating wasteful spending on ineffective marketing, as well as leveraging advertising campaigns that prove the most profitable. By providing "all-in-one" automated systems that allow for the real-time tracking of each generated lead, a business can easily access valuable marketing data with just a few keystrokes.

Richard's marketing expertise is regularly sought out by the media, which he's shared on NBC, CBS, ABC and FOX affiliates, as well as in *The Wall Street Journal, USA Today* and *Newsweek*. He's also launched his own television show, "ROI TV," which features interviews with other top marketing specialists.

To learn more about Richard Seppala, The ROI Guy™, and how you can receive free special reports and other invaluable marketing information from one of the country's leading experts, visit www.YourROIGuy.com or call Toll-Free 1-800-647-1909.

CHAPTER 11

EARN YOUR WAY INTO THE HEARTS & MINDS OF YOUR CUSTOMERS

BY LUBA WINTER

"He who has a thing to sell
And goes and whispers down a well
Is not so apt to get the dollars
As he who climbs a tree and hollers"

– Author Unknown

The point is, you may have the greatest product or service in the world, but if no one knows about it, who cares? In order to succeed, you simply must market yourself, your product or your service, especially these days. The challenge is how to win the hearts and minds of the vast masses and persuade them that they should buy whatever it is you are selling.

GETTING THEIR ATTENTION

I grew up in the Ukraine, where rich farmland is as abundant as the many folk tales having to do with the rural life. The story is told of a farmer who wanted to buy a mule from his neighbor. The price seemed fair so he asked his neighbor if the mule was obedient and could plow well.

"This mule will do anything you ask," the neighbor said. "All you have to do is speak to him gently."

The farmer bought the mule, intending to put him to work the next day plowing a field. When the mule had been hitched up, the farmer flicked the reins across the big animal's back and said "Поїхали!," which is Ukrainian for "Go!" But the mule didn't move. The farmer tried talking softly and kindly to the mule, as he had been instructed, giving him all kinds of commands, all of which meant, "Please plow now," but to no avail. Finally he called his neighbor, who came over immediately. When he heard the problem, the neighbor picked up a nearby sturdy tree limb and hit the mule in the head. Then he whispered a command in the mule's ear, and the mule began to plow, making deep, straight furrows in the dark, rich soil. When the field was finished, the farmer went back to his neighbor for an explanation.

"You said that all I had to do was speak gently to the mule," said the farmer.

"Well," answered the neighbor, "You just have to get his attention first."

The key to successful marketing in the 21st century is getting the attention of the consumer. That is no easy task. The attention-grabbing efforts of the modern media remind me of a swarm of reporters and photographers clamoring for the attention of celebrities entering a movie premiere. "Over here! Over here!" they seem to shout, waving urgently at their prey. Advertisers have bombarded the airwaves and flooded the pages of magazines with every kind of approach imaginable. The assault on the eyes and ears of the consumer has resulted in a smug aloofness that is becoming more and more difficult to penetrate. The buying public has insulated itself against the cacophony of jingles and slogans with a cool indifference, as if to say, "Go ahead (yawn)…give it your best shot. But I'm pretty hard to impress."

WHY CLEVER WORKS AND YELLING DOESN'T

One recent poll asked television viewers which commercials they liked and disliked the most. Ranking high on the list of the most disliked were those put on the tube by local automobile dealerships. Why? Because they yell. They start the commercial screaming about how they have the "best deals" and how they have "slashed prices to the bone" in order to "beat the competition." Who do they think they are kidding? They can't all have the best deals. And who is the competition? We immediately smell a rat when the claim is made that prices are so low that the reduction in cost will somehow leave the dealership little or profit. When these commercials air, most people tune them out—either literally with the volume knob, or psychologically. Either way, they are simply not effective. And finally, when someone is yelling at you, do you stop and say to yourself, "Wow! They are really making a good point here," or do you just wish they would stop yelling?

Clever, on the other hand, works like a charm. It's not pushy; it's just very "pully." It draws the consumer in through humor, irony, or a catchy phrase. Sam Leith, in his book *Words Are Like Loaded Pistols*, calls rhetoric an art form and makes the observation that a carefully crafted phrase can move the masses. Some advertising phrases roll off the tongue in just such a way as to become instant and enduring classics.

An excellent example of this is the classic line, "Where's the beef?" advertising campaign put out by Wendy's chain of hamburger restaurants in the 1984. At first, the commercial aired with a middle-aged bald man saying, "Thanks, but where's the beef?" That didn't make hamburgers and fries fly off the shelves, but the marketing wizards thought the idea still had legs. They were right. The next series of commercials used the grandmotherly actress Clara Peller, who receives a burger with a massive bun from a fictional competitor which uses the slogan "Home of the Big Bun". The small hamburger patty prompts Peller to angrily exlaim, "Where's the beef?" That one caught the fancy of an American public in startling fashion. The catchphrase began to be repeated on television shows, magazines and films. The most memorable use of the catchphrase was during the Democratic presidential primary debate of March 11, 1984, when former Vice President Walter Mondale attacked his rival, Sen. Gary Hart, by saying, "When I hear your new ideas, I'm reminded of that ad, 'Where's the beef?'"

INBOUND MARKETING

As the term suggests, inbound marketing is the antithesis of outbound marketing. Outbound marketing is when you take it to the people. Inbound marketing is when the people come to you. Outbound marketing is when you are begging and bugging your way in, either through telemarketing, paid advertisements or paying sales people a commission to hawk your wares. Inbound marketing, on the other hand, is based on the idea of earning the attention of your would-be buyers by making yourself easy to be found. Inbound marketing draws potential clients and customers to your product or service. Inbound marketing requires that you make yourself easy to be found through websites, blogs, videos, and podcasts that produce content that consumers value. Inbound marketing is *earning your way in*, letting yourself be found, welcoming those who wish to visit or browse and then converting them to customers through quality offerings. Inbound marketing also places emphasis on allowing your existing customer base to lead you to other clients or customers through referrals or word-of-mouth advertising. High importance is placed on customer satisfaction for this reason.

Since the invention of devices that allow television viewers to skip commercials, guess what? Most do. One poll showed that 86% of viewers skip commercials and 44% of direct mail recipients never open the envelopes. On the other hand, companies that blog and produce useful, interesting content have twice as many website visitors as those who don't. An entire industry has been created that focuses on techniques to attract potential customers to your website.

IT STARTS WITH AN IDEA

For marketing to be effective these days, it has to touch. There has to be that certain spark that emotionally connects you with the mind of the customer. It may be an effort to define exactly what that spark is, just like it is difficult to define what light is. But you know it when you feel it, and it is unmistakable. It is the "Idea" that, that once in motion, collects speed on its own momentum and takes on its own form and space. Most importantly, it can change a company's fortune overnight.

The world of social networking has given us the term "going viral," which is applied to any thing, most often a You Tube video, but could be applied to the rapid proliferation of a joke, a rumor or a catchphrase. For your marketing idea to go viral is the best thing that could happen, if you are in the business of selling something or offering a service. It is the Tsunami of marketing. You stand out in the crowd. You no longer have to take it to the people. The people come to you.

Before you can even begin, however, you have to be crystal clear on exactly what value you bring to the table for our anticipated client base. Sometimes just answering this question can put you in soul searching mode. Myself, I am in cosmetology. What I do is manage a chain of beauty salons across the country. In addition to that I market the Revolution 4G, a device that trims years off the user's appearance by removing wrinkles and smoothing skin. But I was once asked "What is your mission?" I spent the next three days answering that question for myself, because it got to the roots of why I am in business to begin with. Why should people want to know me or what I do if I am incapable of explaining something so basic as why I do it?

I called the individual up who had asked the question and thanked them. I explained how much self examination had gone into the answer, and then I told them my mission was simply to make others feel better about themselves and thereby reach their full potential in life.

What is your mission? Why do you do what you do? Why should people come to you? What makes you, your product or your service unique?

IT'S NOT ABOUT ME, IT'S ABOUT THEE

The screaming automobile dealership pitchman yell, "Come on down to Haversham and Third where the deals are smoking and we're not joking," adding that they are overstocked and they have to move out the old inventory to make way for the new, blah, blah, blah. Oh yes, they are giving away free hot dogs and free balloons. Thanks for the hot dogs and the balloons, but I can't say that I have ever bought anything because I got a free hot dog.

At the roots of whatever it is you are marketing has to come the mantra, "It's not about me, it's all about thee." *A brand can be a powerful thing if it is about the customer, not the company.* Nike has a logo that is called the "Swoosh." It looks like a fat check mark. Nothing about the logo says "shoes" or any other piece of athletic equipment. They have distinguished themselves in the marketplace by touting how their products enhance the performance of those who use them. No one cares about the type of leather or cloth or rubber used in the making of the product itself. So Nike doesn't concentrate its marketing on those mundane things. Instead, they focus on how the use of their product makes the user better, often tossing into the mix some lofty profundity about personal achievement that puts the marketing on a much higher plane than mere merchandising.

Most recently, McDonalds has introduced into its marketing program scenes of ordinary people meeting at their favorite McDonalds restaurant for conversation. They may be selling hamburgers and egg muffins, but their focus is on the people and the conversations they have. Nowhere does the marketing piece get into the freshness of their fries or the juiciness of their burgers. That is old school stuff. They are striving to create that synapse between the product and the people by focusing on the people. Nice touch.

A powerful brand is one that builds a reputation in the mind of the customer of a company, product or service that help makes them who they are. It is so relevant to them personally that it becomes a symbol of who they are. They wear Chanel No. 5 cologne, brush with Colgate toothpaste, wear Manolo Blahnik shoes, Calvin Klein jeans and drive a BMW. That's who they are. Serve them well and you are likely to do business with their friends and your profits will grow exponentially. Serve them poorly, and you will lose the lot of them.

A great brand has staying power. They may change a lot of things in their life, but they will hang onto the brand because it defines them. Price? Sure it's important. But it certainly isn't the only thing involved, and in many cases it ranks way back there on the scale of importance. The proper combination of price and value becomes a powerful marketing force that can be irresistible to the public. A grocery chain by the name of Trader Joe's has an entire aisle of their store dedicated to wines. They have wine buyers who make huge deals with vineyards to bring the best wine for the buck to the table. One of their wines is from the Charles Shaw vineyard, which makes a palatable Cabernet Sauvignon which Trader Joe's sells for $2.95

per bottle. They can't keep it on the shelves now that it has become universally known as "Two-Buck Chuck."

HOW ARE WE DOING

I have a friend who loves to fill out comment cards. She will even ask for them sometimes at restaurants and other places where service is rendered. I asked her once why she does it. She told me that in her business, she encourages customer surveys and asks everyone she does business with to fill out a comment card.

"I live and die by these," she told me. "If they are that important to me, I know they will be important to these people."

As it turns out, the comment card she was filling out at this particular restaurant asked patrons to rate the service from poor to excellent and give comments as to why. She had nothing but good things to say about everything from the food to the service, but she did make the tiny observation that the air conditioning had made the room too cool on the day of our visit.

Whether or not her comments made a difference, who know? But it is a fact that asking customers for their input accomplishes two things. It lets them know that you care about their opinion and that it matters to you whether you are meeting their needs. It should also allow you the ability to tweak your offerings so they have more appeal to your customer base. If you consider your customers to be happy ones, then confirm it through surveys and comment cards. Offer a premium for the time and effort they expended filling them in. If people are not happy with the results they received doing business with you, you certainly wish to know that as well, don't you? These activities help you build credibility with your clients and customers.

SAY "THANK YOU" OFTEN AND SINCERELY

It is only natural to want to feel special. We all want to be appreciated and valued. A story that resonates with me is the one about Gary Vaynerchuk, founder of the WineLibrary.com. He once directed his marketing department to follow a customer's tweets from his Twitter account, which is a perfectly legitimate thing to do (I add that because it has come to be known as "Twitter stalking," which sounds rather sinister). They found by following the customer's tweets that he is a huge fan of the Chicago Bears. Many of his tweets were lionizing the then quarterback of the team, Jay Cutler. To thank the man for his first WineLibrary.com order, Vaynerchuk sent him a Bears jersey signed by Cutler. Months later, the customer wrote to Vaynerchuk, thanking him and asking how Vaynerchuk knew to send the jersey. Nice touch. Good marketing.

ABOUT LUBA

Luba Winter – Skin Care Expert, Entrepreneur and Inventor of Rejuvenation G4

Making women and men look better and feel better about themselves is the passion for entrepreneur and inventor, Luba Winter. Winter, an expert in skin care and the founder of Nu Way Beauty, has traveled to various parts of the world to perfect her revolutionary product that brings the technology of high-end spa and dermatological treatments to the home market in a very affordable fashion. With the assistance of top level European engineers and cosmetologists, Winter developed the "Rejuvenation G4" as a home remedy for individuals to care for their skin and to slow the affects of the aging process on one's appearance. Using galvanic, ultrasound and phototherapy treatments in this innovative handheld device has enabled thousands of users to achieve youthful looking results they never imagined possible.

Winter has a strong educational background in dermatology as well as clinical psychology. This interesting combination gives her a unique perspective on how one's outward appearance affects how they feel about themselves and the world around them.

The FDA cleared and patent-pending Rejuvenation G4 was put under rigorous safety testing, including hundreds of clinical study participants performing more than 500 face treatments. A panel of doctors specializing in dermatology and plastic surgery saw a noticeable reduction in wrinkles in ninety-eight percent of participants after only one month of daily treatments. After 12 weeks of galvanic, ultrasonic and phototherapy skin treatments, 94 percent of participants agreed that the Rejuvenation G4 appears to eliminate fine lines, rather than just reduce the appearance of fine lines. Dr. Max Grishkevich, an investigative dermatologist at the VIP MediSpa in Portland, Oregon, ran several comprehensive clinical studies on the Rejuvenation G4. He states, "Blind evaluations revealed improvement in more than ninety percent of the subjects and user satisfaction was high to very high."

Winter has an extremely busy schedule as she continues to expand the market for her Rejuvenation G4 product. She is also launching Nu Way Beauty's Nataliya for Women and Nataliya for Men products. In addition to her work as a skin care expert and product designer, she is the author of *How to Look Beautiful Without Harming Yourself*, to be released later this year. Because of her success she has been invited to write chapters in the upcoming books *Breaking the Success Code* by Brian Tracy and *Marketing Miracles* by Dan Kennedy. She is a sought after speaker and has been featured on radio, has been written about and quoted in publications, and has appeared on *America's Premier Experts* television program. Winter will soon be featured in *USA Today* as one of America's "Game Changers" because of her leadership and expertise in her industry. Winter anticipates her product reaching either QVC or the Home Shopping Network in the near future. She is dedicated to continue developing organic beauty products, educating others, and helping business owners improve their businesses in her industry. Additional information about Winter, Rejuvenation G4, and her other products are available on the company website at www.nuwaybeauty.com.

CHAPTER 12

THE POWER OF A PRICE

BY MIKKEL PITZNER

I am thrilled to have been invited to this book collaboration with Dan Kennedy, a man who comes with legendary reputation for marketing savvy, skills and insights—not to mention results. So in contemplating on what exactly to write about for my personal contribution to this book I came up with "The Power Of A Price."

Let's talk about price. Or pricing. Now, ordinarily speaking, this is an area that does not interest me much; it can actually annoy me at times. For instance, I recently had this beautiful fancy top-model Ferrari (if you must know, this was a brand new Ferrari 599 GTB) and more often than I care to remember, people would ask me: "How much did that cost?" and quite honestly I never really wanted to tell. Quite possibly because I also found it embarrassing just how much money was poured into what is ultimately just a car. I would rather talk about the benefits of the car rather than how much I had to shell out for it.

But there are a couple of exceptions when I find price talks hold particular interesting aspects, and where special considerations may be a key ingredient to actually making the business (or indeed break it).

My contribution, which I hope you will find valuable, will illustrate a couple of strategies you can utilize to set your business on the map in a big way and bring you the results that many others try to accomplish in vain.

Let's dig in straight away.

THE POWER OF FREE

You cannot beat free. Free offers just seem to open up the flood gates of customers pouring in and certain marketers have built their entire customer base and business on a foundation of a free offer. You find this marketing ploy used by almost all online information product marketers and it is their way of obtaining that new potential customer.

They offer some product or piece of information (hopefully a good one, but that actually seems to vary a lot) for free in return for obtaining the name and email address of the potential customer (or some form of contact information). Then once the contact information is in the bag they sometimes present an immediate offer of a complementary product of perhaps an extension and expansion of the product given for free, but this time there is a price to be paid for the offer if the customers chooses to get it.

More and more marketers are finding out, however, that it is more powerful to give away even more great offers or valuable information (often in the form of training videos) for free over a period of time following the sign up or what's often called the opt-in. The reason for this is that they are now establishing rapport and building up trust *before* they move ahead with their real product that comes with a price label attached. It's kind of like taking your prospect out for a few more dates before you move in for the kiss.

It is important to note that just because you are giving away something for free, it still needs to be something with a real (or at least, perceived) value to the recipient. If it doesn't, you more than likely will not be able to sell them anything or keep the prospective customer, but they will opt out and look elsewhere and be altogether turned off by your offerings.

This free price model works wonders in the online market space, but it actually works just as well in the offline market space.

Meeting a lot of people I am often asked what I do, and my reply has usually been that I am a serial entrepreneur. Well, in fact as someone I recently met told me, I am more a *parallel entrepreneur* as I endeavor in multitudes of businesses and enterprises at any one given time. It's how I like it. I enjoy being engaged in many different things and then making use of my experience and expertise from across many areas and different businesses and industries into each enterprise and see how I can bring value to that and increase its potential and real results.

One of such enterprises that I am engaged in is that of a company called Freetrailer. The name says it all, especially when I offer you just a few more specific insights to the company. Freetrailer offers small cargo trailer rentals for FREE. You would know such similar trailers from the small box trailers that you latch onto your car's tow hitch and in which you can transport your goods, purchases, or furniture from one place to another. For example if, you are moving from one location to another, or if you just bought a sofa or a refrigerator and now need to get it home, but cannot fit it into your car and don't want to pay for a delivery service. In the United States of America, you would probably recognize similar trailers from the company called U-Haul, except at U-Haul you actually would have to pay for the rentals—Freetrailer offers them for FREE.

Our business model is that these trailers are advertise-funded. In other words we partner up with big box companies who we call our partners, an example is IKEA. We dress the trailers with the partners' logos and then offer the trailers for rentals at the partners' locations for free while the partner pays us for the advertising which then pays for us bringing the trailers and service about.

The benefit for the big box partner is that they get very targeted advertising out to their very specific target audience while at the same time aiding their customers to an inexpensive way of bringing their purchases home. The partner also actually acquires new customers simply for the fact that the trailers are available from the partner. No purchases are necessary, but since the customer is there anyway to pick up the trailer, they might as well go and look at that bookshelf and the night table lamp they have been thinking about getting. The partner also enjoys great goodwill from the trailer user. Who does not appreciate a partner that makes available a free solution?

So in providing this free service, the partner is acquiring customers, receiving goodwill and gaining customer loyalty while getting the customers to bring their advertising out to the exact areas other potential partner customers reside. The model the partner is utilizing is the Free Price model (or freemium).

In this setup Freetrailer is offering the freemium model too. While Freetrailer makes no money on the model from the advertising which only pays for bringing about the trailers, Freetrailer does make money on small "upsells," such as an extra day's hire or sales of insurance. The price offered for these upsells are so small in comparison to the value that about two-thirds of the trailer users actually end up making use of these offers. Large volumes of trailer usage multiplied by small amounts accumulate to noticeable sums that then pays for our CEO, Key Account Executives, Support personnel, office etc. and leaves us with profits. Currently the Freetrailer model is offered all over Denmark and all over Sweden and will soon come to a city near you.

In closing our discussion of the Free Price offer, there are countless of ways in which a company can utilize this strategy and build a sound business from it. I mentioned the online information product marketers from the online world and Freetrailer from the offline brick and mortar service industry world.

In other words whether your business or your product or service resides in the online or offline world, the free price strategy is one you can utilize to grow, expand and build your business. Who knows? Perhaps yours will be one of the really big ones. Remember the model used by Google and Facebook—just to name some of the very current big company names of today—is the free price model.

THE HIGH TICKET PRICE OFFER

Now at the other end of the price scale is what I call the High Ticket Price Offer. Basically under this positioning ploy you offer your product, service, expertise or information (or whatever you sell), but this time at a very high price.

It is interesting to note the effects of a high ticket price offering. First of all, it instantaneously drives the prospective buyers' interest and curiosity up. Right away when presented with a high ticket price offer on a product or service that resonates with the prospective buyer, questions in their heads start to pile up. Questions such as: "How can it be so expensive?", "Is it really worth this?", "What secrets are revealed that could mean all the difference for me and my own success?", "Can I afford this?" or even "Can I afford not to buy this?"

By utilizing a very high ticket price for your product you accomplish a number of things. With higher and higher price points you automatically siphon off the buyers who quite simply cannot afford your product or your services. And although my altruistic heart would want the best for everybody, not every product or service may be equally suited for everybody and a high ticket price product or service more than likely would be better fitting with someone who has the means to actually buy it. Not to belittle those of few means, but it is very, very often cited that customer support issues seem to diminish with higher product or service prices. In other words, it could appear as if those who tend to buy a high ticket price product or service has a lower propensity to complain or raise many issues.

A high ticket price also instantaneously raises customers' expectation to the product and not least the value a customer will place of said product or service. The latter can be a blessing in itself as the customers automatically perceive the product or service to be of extra high value. The former naturally demands of you to make sure your product or service actually does come with incredibly high value. Indeed sometimes when we are given something for free we often tend to place no value on it and thus as a result often do not make use of it or do not regard it as something really of use. By same token oftentimes when we buy something that came with a high price tag, we tend to value it higher and take better care of it or make better use of it.

The high ticket price also may come with the benefit that you as the buyer will feel like you are special and you now are part of a limited and elite group who had the rare privilege of acquiring the product or service.

So going back to my Ferrari, although I never liked to discuss the high price the car came with, it certainly brought my value placement right up there, where I did not just view the car as just a car, but as a real supercar, but also in the eyes of everybody it also brought me in with a select few who had the privilege and joy of such a vehicle (for better or worse). Was one of my motives for buying such an outrageous car to be recognized as someone not just quite ordinary?

A lot of prestige may be bought with high ticket price products and services. Most recognized luxury brands sell products that while they may be of high quality and standards, certainly come at a much higher price than said product could be sold at while still leaving a decent profit margin. Just think of many of the big luxury names such a Louis Vuiton, Chanel, Hermes and many of the luxury cars etc. People buying these products more often than not are not just buying into good quality, nice product and such, but also buy into the prestige, the look, the fashion, the recognition and not least status they believe they will obtain with the product.

This can be very powerful when selling your product or service.

As mentioned earlier the online world has seen an incredible amount of people and experts selling advice and how-to training, and it is offered at a great variety of prices. So consider the online information product world. Wouldn't you quite possibly believe the product that is offered at $10,000 for a three-day seminar to be so much more valuable than a 3-day seminar that comes with a $3,000 price tag? Would you not automatically also believe the attendees who would come to the two different events might be attendees who already were getting different results? If not, then just exchange the numbers with something of bigger difference, so imagine the Mastermind that comes a $10,000 a year compared to a mastermind offered at $100,000 or hell, for that matter, compare it with one that comes at $1,000,000 a year.

Trust me, I am making no judgments on the people who can afford the different price points. But these price points do exist in the real world and I would suspect (from what I have experienced myself) and hope that the obtained value from each of these programs would differ as well.

Now make no mistake: whatever you sell, you must bring real value to your customer. If you don't, your sales and your success will be short lived. To illustrate the point, allow me to reference one of my own experiences from back when I ran the largest limousine service in Denmark.

Through my limousine service company we were offering high end corporate limousine and professional transportation services to professionals, multinational companies, embassies, royalties, celebrities and even the entourages of presidents including three recent US presidents.

When we had the right team and we knew we delivered second to none service, we also increased our rates, some times way above the rates offered by our competitors. But we got away with it. Our customers perceived we were well worth it and we were, and we also as a result obtained much higher profit margins than those of our competitors.

Unfortunately, by the same token at one point in time our team changed and was no longer the ultimate resource for the services we offered; soon it proved difficult to uphold the prices, especially when forced with market conditions such as world focus on cost savings over service level etc. In fact, due to too long a process of finding a well functioning team again, the pressure on price grew and grew and eventually we entered into one of in my eyes most dreaded situations for any business to be in; the situation where you are really just competing on price.

In my book only companies like the Walmarts that can operate huge volumes should ever engage in competing on price. All other businesses better find other value propositions (at least perceived) than price. It is my contention that if you allow yourself to compete just on price, you are bound to fail, because there is always someone out there willing to offer the same product or service at a lesser price, if for no other reason than because that person cannot make any calculations or omits taking into account his or her own time consumed by supplying the product or service.

Ultimately, our results began to lack and actually running the business became less fun. The clientele seemed to change, too. It was way more fun, not to say lucrative, running the business when our value proposition was in the high ticket price category.

With the right focus and bringing the right value about and you too can enjoy a high ticket price business. Or you may be able to build your business on that intriguing strategy of free or super high value at very low prices and feel really good about bringing something like that to market, while still being greatly compensated. Indeed if you bring the value to market, the market will compensate you.

PRICE JUXTAPOSITION

I wanted to end my contribution to this chapter illustrating another price point strategy that can prove excessively important for your success with selling your product or services, but alas, my contribution is under a space limit here in this book, so I am out of more lines to put in. But fret not, I hope you have really enjoyed my insights on the two ultimate price point strategies and I will give you the insight on Price Juxtaposition to you for free as well, so if you go to my website at www.mikkelpitzner.com/price-juxtaposition, then you can get the continuance of this chapter. Hope to see you there.

ABOUT MIKKEL

Mikkel Pitzner was born on March 3, 1968. He received a Bachelor of Science in Economics from University College of London (England) with honors in 1991. He has completed shorter intense courses in Political Science and Game Theory at Columbia University in New York, and a business course for CEOs at Harvard Business School in Massachusetts.

He is a serial and parallel entrepreneur, investor, and professional board member in Denmark, Sweden and the U.S. (who currently sits on nine boards spanning diverse industries), as well as a marketing and social media expert and consultant, master-minder, and dreamer extraordinaire.

He is a partner in the unique marketing and trailer rental company Freetrailer, which currently operates throughout Denmark and Sweden with more countries to come. He is a partner of Aksel & Ko, a company that can find that special gimmick or solution corporations need for their marketing strategies.

Pitzner is originally from Denmark, where he used to run what became the fourth-largest car rental company and a leasing company whose size he doubled and locations he quadrupled. Until recently, he owned and operated the largest limousine service company in Denmark, whose profits he managed to grow 3200% during the first year of ownership alone. The company served the most discerning clientele, including no fewer than three U.S. presidents—George W. Bush, Bill Clinton and Barack Obama, the last one during the United Nations Climate Change Conference in 2009 during which the company serviced more than 200 limousines to the U.S. Embassy in Copenhagen, along with numerous other embassies, countries, royalties, celebrities, multi-conglomerates, and so on. Pitzner also successfully ran an import and distribution company of scuba diving equipment until that company was sold to a German distributor.

Mikkel Pitzner is also a best-selling author and speaker who teaches entrepreneurs how to create a business that will provide them with the lifestyle they choose while taking them off the treadmill of their jobs. Pitzner has been featured on CNBC, ABC, NBC, CNNMONEY.com, Fox News, CBS News, and in the *Wall Street Journal, Fortune, Fast Company, SmartMoney* and *USA Today*. He was also recently a guest on the "Brian Tracy Show."

Mikkel Pitzner currently resides in Florida with his beautiful wife Olga and 21-month-old son Gabriel, and they're expecting a baby girl. He's building four new business ventures simultaneously, while helping a local manufacturer in a struggling and challenging economy.

CHAPTER 13

EMBRACING ONLINE MARKETING

BY LINDSAY DICKS

We live in the most astounding time when it comes to marketing resources and potential. Not long ago, a small business had very limited reach and it sometimes took years before their marketing reach was able to go beyond their local community. However, in today's environment, a small business can launch and literally reach around the world with their product or service the very same day… a marketing miracle we call the Internet. While that may be an oversimplification of the process, it is not an exaggeration. Granted, certain infrastructure components must be established before the marketing reach can become effective. But the reality is that you no longer have to be a giant business to have a worldwide marketing footprint.

There are many terms used in the virtual world for promoting your business: online marketing, internet marketing, web marketing, webvertising, e-marketing, social media marketing…and the list goes on. Whatever you may call it, if you don't have it or don't use it

139

effectively in your business, you are shortchanging your possibility for growth and expansion. It has been said, "If you don't have an online presence, your business doesn't exist."

Today you can earn an undergraduate or graduate degree in online marketing. However, most online marketers don't carry such a degree. In fact, many very successful online marketers today don't even have a degree of any kind. One of the very interesting things about the digital age is that many online marketing practices are self-taught or accomplished through informal or semi-formal training methods. In recent years there has been a plethora of online marketing efforts geared toward finding individuals that will pay a web-based company to be trained in the art of online marketing through a series of training modules. In other words, people have made a great deal of money training others online to become online marketers.

It would be an understatement to say that internet marketing can become very complex, confusing, and ever changing. What is written today about internet marketing may become old news within a few months. New services are always on the horizon and the next magic application is usually lurking around the corner. Yet, there are some consistent strategies that will continue to be effective as business owners ride the wave of the constantly evolving cyber world. Let's discuss those strategies.

The first question that has to be answered is, "Who is your customer?" You may be surprised to know that many businesses fail to really evaluate their customer base. I often ask business owners about the demographic of their customer base. It is not unusual for the business owner to get a glazed-over look in their eyes and respond with, "I'm not really sure." It is imperative to fully understand your target market if you are going to effectively communicate with them. The way you communicate to a twenty-five year old will be much different than communicating with a sixty-five year old. Information such as age, socio-economic status, geographical location, gender, education, marital status, and social values are key factors in understanding your audience.

Another crucial component to your online marketing effort is Search Engine Optimization (SEO). This can become a daunting task and may be overwhelming for the less tech savvy business owner. You must fine tune your focused content pages and your home page by making certain adjustments to make them rank higher in the search engines. There is software available which enables you to check your current ranking and compare your web pages against your top keyword competitors. The software will also make recommendations for what changes to make. This type of SEO fine tuning can quickly move many people out of their tech comfort level. For that reason, many businesses outsource SEO.

In order to have an effective internet marketing campaign, you must be convinced that taking your business into the cyber world is an investment and not an expense. While we all understand the checks you write to pay for an internet presence has to come from the debit side of your bank account, it is imperative that you recognize the return on investment that will follow. Until you are able to grasp this concept, you will not commit the necessary resources to make your online presence effective. If you don't have an effective online presence, it won't deliver desired results and you will conclude that your attempt at internet marketing was a failure. Don't set yourself up for failure. Make sure you have a commitment to online marketing. Don't be afraid to move some of your traditional marketing budget to be used for online marketing efforts. While online marketing doesn't have to be extremely expensive, there will be some costs to an effective campaign.

There are numerous online marketing tools that can be used. However, if you try to use too many of these tools you will water down your efforts and become ineffective. Focus on four or five tools with which you feel confident and master them. If you are new to online marketing don't be afraid to ask others that have more experience. Seek out other business owners that have used internet marketing strategies effectively and ask them why they use those tools and how it has impacted their business. There are also many internet marketing consultants who can give you guidance in creating a strong online presence for your business. While the consultants will charge for their services, they may prove to be one of your best allies in business. However, make sure you do your due diligence when selecting a consultant. I would recommend you talk to others who have used the consultant and ask very detailed questions about the consultant-business owner relationship and the effectiveness of their work.

This leads us to a very important topic. Should you take care of your internet marketing in-house or should you outsource that task? There are varying opinions on this subject by the experts. But, here is a general rule of thumb. If you can accomplish effective internet marketing internally, then you should keep it in-house where you have the most control over the activity. However, if you cannot manage your internet marketing effectively in-house, you should outsource it. The key word here is "effectively." Many businesses have an ineffective in-house online marketing presence which is not benefiting them. Depending on the size of your business and the size of your marketing strategy, it may be less expensive to outsource. To accomplish online marketing effectively internally, you will have to hire someone experienced in online marketing, offer them a competitive wage, benefits, vacation time, and pay employee taxes and unemployment expenses. Then, you pray they don't ever get upset with something on the job and walk out on you, leaving you with no one controlling your online presence. While you do maintain more control by having in-house staff, there are also some inherent risks. On the other hand, if you outsource, you don't have to worry about the overhead expenses or worry about your online marketer suddenly quitting or taking an extended leave of absence.

You may want to begin with very stable, tried and vetted tools as you begin your online marketing strategy. Even businesses that have been marketing online for many years often will stick with these venues. The most common online marketing avenues used by businesses today continue to be Facebook, Twitter, Youtube, e-newsletters, and blogs. As of this writing, the venues that seem to be gaining the most traction and continuously growing in popularity and usage are Pinterest and mobile applications. Of course, there are many other resources that can be used but the list would become too lengthy to outline here. After you narrow your focus on the online services you will use in your marketing campaigns and strategy, it is very important to have a specific plan and to work your plan consistently. I cannot stress enough the importance of having a specific plan and working the plan consistently.

The entire goal for your online marketing campaign must be to drive people to your website and to your business. Marketing, of course, is for the end goal of increasing sales and the resulting increase in gross revenue. You increase sales by building relationships and creating exuberant interest in your product or service through online marketing. One of the ways you create relationships and build exuberant interest is by offering something free. People love to receive free "stuff." Giving something free does not necessarily have to be a product that costs you large amounts of money. It can be free information. You may want to create white papers about a specific subject that will be of interest to your target market then make it known through your online marketing venues that you have free, downloadable information that will be of benefit to them. Or, you may want to give away a product or service so you can drive attention to your business. For example, if you have an auto detailing shop, why not run a contest to offer a free deluxe auto detailing service to the person that has brought in the most new fans to your Facebook fan page? You will create a buzz about your business, you will create new relationships and build on the existing relationships, you will create exuberant interest in your service, and one of your Facebook fans will become one of your most loyal customers because you gave them something "free!"

Let's talk about the new social media kid on the block and how businesses are using it to promote themselves. Pinterest is a social image bookmarking site that has experienced phenomenal growth since its inception in 2009. According to some reports, as of this writing, it is the third most popular social network only to be topped by Facebook and Twitter. Only six months ago it was in the number seven spot. The site hit ten million monthly unique U.S. visitors faster than any other site in the history of the internet. You might think of Pinterest as a form of "window shopping" for anything that may appeal to you or catch your interest. It may be a physical item such as clothing, furniture, or a vehicle. Or, it may be pictures of exotic vacation spots or a cluster of your favorite quotes. Individuals using this site will "pin" their selections to their board and others can follow them to see what they have pinned. The pinning process is also conveniently tied to Facebook or Twitter so more of your friends can also share the experience with you.

Where there is an application, businesses must find a way to use it for marketing purposes. Pinterest has been no exception. Businesses use

Pinterest because it is exploding in popularity, it is constantly adding new users and it has the ability to drive traffic and build your SEO. Since images are at the heart of Pinterest, make sure your photos are high quality and that they are tagged correctly so they index properly within Pinterest. Encourage comments about your pins by asking questions such as, "Tell us about your experience using our new product." You can also imbed pins into your blog. One good way to get more followers is to follow other pinners. They will then often follow you in return. Make sure you create key words or hash tags for your pins to optimize your pins for people that search for pins by key words. It is very important that you always link back to your website in your Pinterest profile to encourage traffic and increase SEO. If you are interested in knowing who is pinning about your business on their board, you can find out by using this specific URL: http://pinterest. com/source/**ADD YOUR URL HERE**. For example: http://pinterest. com/source/abccompany.com.

Blogging is another great opportunity to show the world your expertise, but, it also has another benefit. It can be used effectively to boost your SEO. If you offer excellent content, other users are likely to link to it, thereby increasing your page rank on the search engines. Consistency and content are extremely important when blogging. As with any online content, make sure you have key words strategically placed within your writing to boost SEO. There are also services that will push your blog to numerous sites where it will potentially remain for many months.

Social media sources will be key factors to your online marketing efforts. Facebook is the most commonly used social media venue. Businesses create fan pages and develop strategies to build their fan base. Links to your fan page should be placed on your website, blog, e-mail signature line, and any other electronic medium you may use. Consistency is also very important when communicating with your fan base. Typically, businesses will have daily posts and many businesses will post two to four times a day. Your Facebook posts can also be directly linked to your Twitter account.

Twitter, the second most used social media venue, is a powerful tool. Let me give you a great example of how Twitter can be influential in business. I was talking to a business owner recently who told me about a twitter interaction he had with someone. The business owner was very interested in a reality television program he saw on a popular national television network that featured a certain business industry in which he was intimately involved. The program peaked his interest as a possible way to promote his product to a national audience. Armed with only the name of the program and the name of the host, he began searching through social media sources for contact information. Without much effort he found the host on Twitter. The business owner sent a tweet to the host about his product that could be used on the reality show. Much to his surprise, the host tweeted him back immediately. They continued their tweeting dialogue, which resulted in further non-Twitter discussion. The end result was that in a matter of weeks a contract was signed and the business owner's product is now going to be featured in the reality program that will be aired nationally sometime this summer. Do not underestimate the power of the Tweet!

Online marketing can become very complex. But, it can also become very powerful and result in increased business and increased gross revenue. One thing is for sure: in today's world, your business will not thrive without embracing it.

ABOUT LINDSAY

Lindsay Dicks helps her clients tell their stories in the online world. Being brought up around a family of marketers, but a product of Generation Y, Lindsay naturally gravitated to the new world of online marketing. Lindsay began freelance writing in 2000 and soon after launched her own PR firm that thrived by offering an in-your-face "Guaranteed PR" that was one of the first of its type in the nation.

Lindsay's new media career is centered on her philosophy that "people buy people." Her goal is to help her clients build a relationship with their prospects and customers. Once that relationship is built and they learn to trust them as the expert in their field, then they will do business with them. Lindsay also built a patent-pending process that utilizes social media marketing, content marketing and search engine optimization to create online "buzz" for her clients that helps them to convey their business and personal story. Lindsay's clientele span the entire business map and range from doctors and small business owners to Inc 500 CEOs.

Lindsay is a graduate of the University of Florida. She is the CEO of CelebritySites™, an online marketing company specializing in social media and online personal branding. Lindsay is also a multi-best-selling author including the best-selling book *Power Principles for Success,* which she co-authored with Brian Tracy. She was also selected as one of America's PremierExperts™ and has been quoted in *Newsweek,* the *Wall Street Journal, USA Today, and Inc.* magazine as well as featured on NBC, ABC, and CBS television affiliates speaking on social media, search engine optimization and making more money online. Lindsay was also recently brought on FOX 35 News as their Online Marketing Expert.

Lindsay, a national speaker, has shared the stage with some of the top speakers in the world, such as Brian Tracy, Lee Milteer, Ron LeGrand, Arielle Ford, David Bullock, Brian Horn, Peter Shankman and many others. Lindsay was also a Producer on the Emmy-nominated film Jacob's Turn.

You can connect with Lindsay at:

Lindsay@CelebritySites.com

www.twitter.com/LindsayMDicks

www.facebook.com/LindsayDicks

CHAPTER 14

MAKING A REAL ESTATE MARKETING MIRACLE:

16 SECRET NINJA TECHNIQUES FOR SUCCESS

BY JASON CIANFLONE

When it comes to real estate marketing, literally *everything* has been done...from social networking to bus bench signs, from video to some really crazy, out there guerilla marketing strategies.

The problem is, for a lot of real estate agents, those strategies aren't really working.

Most people get into the real estate industry with high hopes and big dreams, and then wind up failing so completely and spectacularly that they end up getting out *within just two years or make meager living.*

The reason? They never learned how to market themselves properly.

Whether you're a real estate newbie or a battle-hardened veteran, there *is* a secret to becoming a star in your market.

It's all about marketing the right product—*you*. It's all about making yourself into a recognizable, respected, and exciting brand that people know about and want to do business with.

How do you do that? Here are 16 killer Ninja Real Estate Marketing Techniques guaranteed to help you reach the top in *your* market.

TECHNIQUE #1: CREATE YOUR USP

Why should a person choose to do business with you, as opposed to some other agent? It all comes down to your USP.

USP stands for "Unique Selling Proposition"—and yours will make you stand out from the pack. Your USP should be all about what makes you special, what makes you *you*. Working for a brokerage is not a USP—many, many agents do that. Having a real estate license is clearly not a USP. Even being a top negotiator is not a USP, since today, everyone claims to be a top negotiator!

Instead, look for something personal that makes you stand out from the crowd you're competing with. Maybe it's a look—something about the car you drive, or the way you dress that makes you instantly identifiable as "that guy" or "that gal" that everyone wants to work with. Or maybe it's the personal service you provide to all your clients.

In the Jason Cianflone Real Estate Team, our USP is that we are a genuine family operation. We're a close-knit group of Italians—cousins, uncles, even my dad—who spend holidays together, eat pasta together, support each other and work together. Everyone in our area knows the Cianflone family and knows we stand for quality real estate representation.

TECHNIQUE #2: DEFINE YOUR BRAND

Is your brand professional? Is it fun? Is it young? Is it geared toward luxury properties, starter homes, or older clients? You need to figure out what your brand focus is all about, and then choose the colors, typefaces, and imagery that best represent that brand. Keep in mind that when you create a brand that works with your USP, they reinforce each other and make them both stronger.

Our USP is all about how our family takes care of *your* family. So, in all of our branding—our business cards, our ads, our listing signs—we feature our entire family. Yes, it's a lot of people to squeeze onto one little sign, but we do it because *that's who we are.*

TECHNIQUE #3: DRESS FOR SUCCESS

Some real estate agents try to dress like their clients. I advise you to dress for success. A home is the biggest investment most people will ever make, so it's important to look like a knowledgeable, professional expert that clients will feel that they can trust. A good three-piece suit will make you look like the expert you are.

TECHNIQUE #4: ENJOY THE GREAT OUTDOORS

Once you solidify your USP and your brand, it's time to put them to use where everyone can see them. You want people to see your face, your name and your call to action—and of course, your phone number—so often that they become ingrained in their brains.

Outdoor advertising is a fantastic way to make that happen. Bus benches are often the best and most affordable option, but others like to invest in larger signs. Whichever way you go, remember your ultimate goal is to gain maximum visibility with your signs so people see you on their way to and from work, shopping or other leisure activities. That way YOUR brand and YOUR name and YOUR call to action become so ingrained in their brains that when they need a real estate agent—guess who pops into their head?

TECHNIQUE #5: PLAY THE NUMBERS GAME

Every real estate agent has listing signs, but you can make your impact with what you put *on* the sign. A big opportunity is, believe it or not, your phone number. Don't use your broker's number—everyone does that. Instead, get your own number and try to make it something memorable so that it sticks with people. For instance, our number is made up of almost all sevens. When you compare the simple pattern of our number against everyone else's random collection of digits that can be impossible to remember without writing it down, we're already ahead of the game. And we make sure we *stay* ahead by putting the number on the sign two or three times, so you can't possibly miss it.

TECHNIQUE #6: CREATE ATTENTION-GETTING ADVERTISING

We're the first to admit it—we like to go over the top with our ads. We make an open house or a new listing a major event, with lines like "Sale starts NOW!" and "Call me now, don't delay!" And then we usually add some type of giveaway to ramp up the fun factor even more— such as, "Get a Free TV with Your Purchase!" or "Buy This House and We'll Send You to Vegas!" Sometimes we co-brand with other people, offering such "prizes" as a Home Depot shopping spree.

And of course, we always prominently feature our telephone number!

TECHNIQUE #7: BE A RADIO STAR

A lot of real estate agents would never consider advertising on the radio. But when it comes to getting your personality out there, you can't beat it.

Radio lets you speak directly to people, in your own voice, often very inexpensively. Remember, when you do run a radio ad, to include a call to action, and also your phone number, your name, your brand, and any giveaway or offer you've added on.

By the way, radio can also offer FREE advertising opportunities. Depending on where you live, you may be able to win a spot on a "Meet the Experts" panel on a regular radio informational show, or you might even be able to host your own weekly half-hour or hour. Smaller stations are always looking for free programming to fill up air time, and you never know how far a little creativity can take you.

TECHNIQUE #8: BE A VIDEO STAR

I am a huge fan of YouTube videos to market yourself and your business, with one major caveat—you have to do them *the right way.* That means sending links out to your database and using software that will let you market to those people again and again. It's almost like putting out a newscast directly targeted to your prospects week after week.

And, by the way, don't forget a video is most effective when it's entertaining. For example, I posted a video showing me making my grandmother's famous recipe for homemade meatballs. People see me in the kitchen, wearing an apron, having a glass of vino, and it's a whole other side of me. I become a fun guy they want to know and I also share a delicious recipe. The idea is to create value with your marketing, so that people look forward to seeing what you're doing and want to get to know the man or woman behind the image.

TECHNIQUE #9: BE SMART ABOUT SOCIAL MEDIA

Just about everyone in the real estate business is Tweeting, Facebooking and Linking In. But are they actually getting anything out of all that effort?

Using social media effectively means *deciding in advance* what you are going to talk about and making sure it reinforces your brand. Do you think your clients really care about what you ate for breakfast, or that you bought a pair of shoes today? Sure, everyone posts this stuff, but... so what?

My advice is, if you're going to use social media, take the time to come up with something that's interesting, or exciting and informative. Also, when it comes to social media, less is more. Instead of blasting out 70 meaningless updates a day, send out one consistent message, like a tip, a funny news item or anything that adds value or brings a smile to people's faces.

Always make them look forward to hearing from you.

TECHNIQUE #10: GO DOOR TO DOOR

Yes, I know, it sounds old school. But I believe knocking on doors is even more important than ever, since we hardly ever see people face-to-face anymore. In real estate, getting your face out there is everything and many agents fail to make the effort to do that.

The minute you sell a property in your area, seize the moment, print up some flyers, grab a bundle of lollipops or chocolates for the kids, and hit the streets. Introduce yourself to the homeowner, tell them about the property you sold in their area, and let them know that if they need anything, you're there to help. And, of course, give the kids some candy (if it's okay with Mom and Dad).

Let's be real. Chances are the homeowner is not going to say, "Whoa! Dude! I was just thinking of selling my house. Let me list with you right now!" When they ARE ready to buy or sell, however—or one of their friends or relatives is—they'll remember that you were the guy (or gal) who actually took the time to stop by!

And don't forget to ask the people you meet if they'd like to receive your free newsletter to stay updated on local trends and events. That way, you can put them on your mailing list and market to them in other ways.

TECHNIQUE #11: GO PUBLIC

Whether you volunteer to throw out the first pitch at a local baseball game or emcee a charity auction, another way to meet the public is to go out in public. You don't have to go to every Boy Scout Jamboree or Kiwanis Club meeting, but making an appearance at an event at least once a month is something to shoot for. This activity expands your circle of influence and makes people more likely to like and trust you.

TECHNIQUE #12: THROW A PARTY

Who doesn't love parties? Chances are, your clients do (especially if food and drink is on the house!)

So treat them to an occasional fun, social evening. Every three months or so, throw a seasonal bash—a holiday party, a summer barbeque, whatever suits the season. Invite two or three hundred of your closest friends, clients and business associates, take off your tie, slip into your "Kiss the Cook" apron or get behind the bar, and just have a blast. People will remember you for the great time that you showed them and that you gave back to them for giving you their business.

TECHNIQUE #13: STAY IN TOUCH

As your business grows, you may start getting bigger, more important clients—corporate contracts, condo projects, and new home developments. That means you may lose touch with those individuals with which you built your business. Make sure you communicate with them to let them know you're still around and still there for them whenever they need you. A newsletter is a great way to keep them in the loop and to stay top of mind.

TECHNIQUE #14: STATE YOUR MISSION

What are you all about? What matters to you? Your mission statement says it all. And a great place to put that statement is right on the back of your business card. With one glance, your contact or client will know exactly who you are, what you care about and how you're there to help them.

I personally have a separate business card—my so-called "personal business card"—with my home phone number on the back. When I hand it to someone, I tell the person to feel free to call and leave a message (unless it's an emergency), and then later, I call them from home. I'll even have a sit down with them if they want to stop by the house.

TECHNIQUE #15: YOU GIVE AND YOU GET

Never underestimate the power of a move-in gift. Whenever one of your clients moves into a house, make it a point to personally drop by with a thoughtful, well-chosen moving present. And make it a gift that will *last*, not something that will only be around for a few days like fruit or flowers, that way it will continue to remind them of you and your generosity for years to come.

One of my personal favorite gifts to give is a knife set. I know, some people say it's bad luck to give knives, but my executive assistant gave me one and, for me, it was the best gift in the world, because I love to cook. It showed me that she cared about me and what I value. It's also engraved with her name on the bottom, so every time I use it, it reminds me that she gave it to me. Send that kind of message to your clients, and they'll come back to you again and again.

TECHNIQUE #16: DO YOUR WEBSITE RIGHT!

These days, just having a "brochure" website isn't going to cut it. Your website needs to be about more than buying, selling and your personal information. Instead, strive to create a flexible website that is constantly changing with new and valuable information. Include updates on the market, area schools, local sports teams, events in the area, the weather…whatever people care about and might find interesting.

When you provide information like this, it shows that you care about your community. You may need an assistant who can spend an hour or two a day keeping the website up to date, but it's well worth the expense.

OH...AND ONE MORE THING...

The most important Ninja Marketing Technique of all is making sure all the pieces of everything you do *work together*. That builds a unified picture of you and your real estate services and enables you to make the biggest possible impact in your local market.

When you sell yourself correctly, when you train and grow as a professional, when you reach to provide the best service you can to your clients, you become your own best advertisement. Once you reach that tipping point, you can go anywhere and be successful, because you've mastered the essentials and put them all together to make the right things happen.

I wish you all the best in creating your own Real Estate Marketing Miracle!

ABOUT JASON

Jason Livio Franco Cianflone, better known as "The Real Estate Doctor" is a Leader and Innovator in Real Estate Marketing, Advertising, Project Consulting and Investments. Founded on the principle of genuine, caring, personal service, he will consistently exceed all customer expectations, providing a memorable experience and exceptional value. Jason has been seen on NBC, CBS, ABC and Fox affiliates as well as in *The Wall Street Journal, USA Today* and *Newsweek*.

Jason has grown at a remarkable pace in the past 5 years to be known as one of the top in North America and continues to spread nationwide like wild fire. There's no stopping at just buying or selling homes. With a growing team of rising experts and a reputation of excellence including a client base treated like family, Jason continues to strive to provide the best service and advice from Marketing to Project Consulting and more!

To "get to know" Jason Cianflone on a more personal basis and to extend your knowledge in the Real Estate World, visit www.JASONCIANLFLONE.com or call 1-204-772-7777.

www.JASONCIANFLONE.com

CHAPTER 15

MARKETING MIRACLE FORMULA:

5 PRINCIPLES TO SUCCESS

BY LAMONT STEPHENS

When discussing Marketing Miracles, it seems appropriate to consider the marketing principles contained in the historical record of a literal miracle—in the chronological accounts of the kings within the dynasty of Israel, sometime between 536 and 562 BC. The account discusses the plight of a widow of a prominent and well respected individual within his community and probably within quite a wide geographical region. However, while the widow's husband was well respected, he incurred considerable debt prior to his death. Subsequent to his demise, the widow had no means to pay back the debt and was poor, destitute, and was under the obligation to pay the entire debt to the creditor. In the historical setting of the culture in which this narrative occurs, people borrowed money based upon their personal credit, and the primary security for the debt was their own value as a laborer and the value of the labor of their children. If full payment of the debt could not be paid at the time it was due, the debtor and their children became a servant to the creditor to literally "work off" the debt. This was the situation this widow faced. The creditor had called for the debt to be paid, but since there was no money, the creditor was going to take her children into his custody until they worked off the debt.

In desperation, the woman sought out the help of another well respected and authoritative figure within the community. The man's name was Elisha. Elisha engaged the widow in conversation to assess the gravity of the situation and to determine what could be done. He basically asked her two questions. The first, "What do you want me to do?" The second question was, "What do you have in your house?" The answer to the first question is probably obvious. The widow wanted direction from him so she could find a way to pay the debt so her children would not be subject to forced labor. However, the answer to the second question left the woman feeling very inadequate. Literally, the only thing she had in her home was a small amount of oil. Not even enough oil to use in the preparation of a meal. Her response was, "I have nothing in my house except for a little oil."

Without hesitation, Elisha instructed her to go through the neighborhood and collect as many bottles as possible. Not just a few, but as many bottles as the neighbors would give her. She did as she was instructed and brought the bottles inside her home. Elisha then instructed her to take her sons into the house, close the door, and begin pouring the little bit of oil she had into the empty jars until all the jars were full. The widow did as she was instructed and found that the little bit of oil she had seemed to be never ending. She filled jar after jar after jar until every jar was full. **When she no longer had any empty jars, the oil she used also ran out**.

The oil the widow possessed after this miracle was very valuable. She had the opportunity to sell the oil, possibly to some of the same neighbors that gave her the empty bottles as well as others. She would have been able to collect enough money to pay off her debt, keep her sons from forced labor under her creditor, and have enough left over to provide for herself and her children.

There are five principles I see in this account of the miracle that transpired to transform the life and circumstances of this widow. First, there had to be "**motivation**" to change her circumstances. She was in a desperate situation. It's very interesting to see how negative circumstances can become a motivating factor in our lives. Many who are reading this chapter are facing circumstances that seem insurmountable and overwhelming. You may feel like you are suffocating from the burden of your situation and you don't know where to turn or what to do. But, in the midst of the emotional upheaval in your life there is something that stirs within you that says, "I must survive! I must fight through this circumstance!" I'm sure you have heard the phrase used many times, "You can allow your circumstances to make you bitter or better." Even though that expression may be overused at times, there is tremendous truth in it. Listen to the voice inside you that won't allow you to give up. No matter how low you get or how financially destitute you become, don't allow yourself to succumb to the burden of your circumstances. Some of you have a dream to do something really big, but you are surrounded by people that keep telling you it can't be done. It may be your spouse, a family member or a close friend telling you to give up and focus your attention on something more stable or less visionary. Whatever your circumstances may be, use it as catalyst to motivate yourself toward accomplishment.

The second principle contained in the widow's miracle is "**mission**." The widow's mission was to get out of debt and save her children from becoming the forced laborers of her creditor. What is your mission? Have you defined it? The widow knew exactly what she wanted to accomplish, she just wasn't sure how to get there. For me as well as for many others reading this chapter, just like the widow, the welfare of our family and our children is one of our highest priorities in our lives. They become a large part of our mission even though our mission may extend beyond our immediate family. What example would you like to be to your children? Do you want them to see an example of success and accomplishment? I know you're not fighting to keep them from becoming a forced laborer to your creditor like the widow. But, are you a slave to your creditors? Do you have to work day after day and sometimes more than one job just to keep your creditors paid? If so, you have become a slave to your creditors. That is not the example you want to be for your children. Defining your mission will enable you to begin putting into action a plan to break out of negative circumstances and become free from creditors and those issues in life that prevent you from excelling. It is vitally important to have a specific mission in place.

The third principle I see in the widow's miracle is the "**map**" or plan that was provided for her. Did you notice in the historical record of this event that Elisha did not give the widow the entire plan at once? He gave her a simple instruction. He told her to go and gather as many empty bottles as she could possibly find. You may note that the instruction was very simplistic and within her ability to accomplish. There is a key here that must not be overlooked. Some people think that great accomplishment must be done through complex instruction. On the contrary, great accomplishment is usually achieved through a series of very routine, but very consistent steps. Many people think they really have to be stretched and do things that are far outside of their comfort zone to be successful. I'm not suggesting that we should never move outside our comfort zone, in fact, at some point it will be necessary to stretch and grow to achieve significant accomplishment. But, it is even more important to begin doing things that are well within the realm of your zone of comfort and ability. Begin there, where you are most comfortable. Get some successes under your belt. Can you imagine the motivation the widow must have felt when the first neighbor gave her the first bottle as she began her collection? Maybe that neighbor gave her ten bottles. Be assured, there were some neighbors that told her to go away and gave her nothing. But, as long as she was able to see some accomplishment and she kept her eye on her mission, her motivation soared. She followed through on a very simple first step, had a sense of great accomplishment, and was ready for the next step.

The next step in the "map" or plan Elisha laid out for the widow was to begin pouring the small amount of oil into the empty jars she collected. As she poured the oil something miraculous began to happen. It continued to pour out until all the empty jars were completely full. In order for the widow to see the great success of having an overflowing abundance of oil at her disposal she had to follow the map Elisha gave her. It probably didn't make sense in her own mind to begin pouring the little bit of oil she had into an empty jar. But, she followed the instruction in detail and saw things happen that were beyond her comprehension.

Can you imagine what the situation would have been like if she failed to remember the little bit of oil she had in her house? She could have thought the amount of oil was so insignificant that it wouldn't make any difference in her circumstances. That is not unlike how many people think. They look at their resources and determine they don't have anything that can make a difference. Or they fail to see the resources at hand because they are so focused on their circumstances. I remember a story someone told me one time about running into a friend on the street and this individual asked the friend how he was doing. The friend responded, "Alright, under the circumstances." The individual responded, "Well, what are you doing under there?" The friend replied, "Under where?" to which the individual responded, "Under your circumstances." I must ask you that same question. What are you doing under your circumstances? You must get out from under your circumstances where you can see clearly or you might not remember the little bit of oil that has the potential to become the resource to lead you to great victories.

The fourth principle I see is "**marketing**." She initially went to her neighbors to ask for empty bottles. I equate this to building a list. Any marketer knows you have to have a list and you need to keep the list growing. You need to keep prospects continually flowing into your sales funnel. After the widow experienced the miracle of an overflowing abundance of oil, she was able to take her resource to market. While this is purely an assumption on my part, I believe she took her oil back to the same neighbors she contacted for the empty bottles, told them her story, and they began buying. She probably sold oil to neighbors and friends that told her she would never make it. You know those family and friends I'm talking about. She turned oil into cash, paid off her debt and began to live a comfortable life.

The fifth and final principle I see is need for a "**mentor**." While she didn't realize it at the time, the widow had a mentor that would be one of the most renowned historical figures in the annals of time for her nation. Elisha was a man fully qualified to help her out of her circumstances. As a mentor, he listened to her problem and gave her a recommended action plan. The widow had a choice to make. She could follow her mentor's advice or walk away from the advice and try to figure out a solution on her own. Even though her mentor's solution may not have made sense to her at the time, she trusted him and followed his advice. She took a step of faith and believed in the person giving her the advice. Had she not followed his advice, she would have lost her children to her creditor. She would have failed to be an example of success to her children and others around her. But, instead she followed the instruction of her mentor without question and was lead to success. The importance of a qualified mentor cannot be overstressed. If you want to be successful, find someone that is more successful than you and follow their lead. Listen to their advice even when it may not make complete sense to you. Put your confidence in the fact that they have been successful and can lead you down that same path of accomplishment.

The five principles that will guide you to success include:

1. **Motivation** – Don't fall prey to your circumstances, but allow your circumstances to become a motivating factor for you to succeed.

2. **Mission** – Make sure your mission is clear in your mind and that it permeates your entire being.

3. **Map** – Establish a well thought-out plan for yourself and how you will accomplish your mission. Then, follow the map with consistency.

4. **Marketing** – Keep the sales funnel full at all times. Continuously reach out to new prospects.

5. **Mentor** – Find a mentor that is fully qualified and has demonstrated success. Listen intently to what they tell you and trust them.

I have found by following these principles I have accomplished many things in my life that would normally seem to be out of my reach. You can be successful! I believe in you! Believe in yourself! Miracles do happen!

ABOUT LAMONT

Lamont Stephens, also known as "the preacher", is a best-selling author, speaker, entrepreneur, marketing, and business coach, who is sought out regularly for his expertise. Lamont is known for identifying hidden talents and resources within his clients and help them leverage that knowledge in the form of products. He founded Teach By DVD, Inc. in 2007, a company that produces and provides informational products nationwide. Teach By DVD, Inc. helps clients to develop their business through informational product creation and marketing.

Critically acclaimed, Lamont Stephens' "Product Money System"™ allows you start right where you are to create great looking products, put into a marketing system for both offline and online. There is no other easy to use system that takes you step-by-step on how he has created product after product.

To learn more about Lamont Stephens, and how you can receive the free Special Report "Business Success Guide: 5 Foundational Principles for Every Business", visit www.LamontStephens.com or call Toll-Free 1-888-DVD-Income (1-888-383-4626).

www.LamontStephens.com

CHAPTER 16

HOW TO TURN WEBSITE VISITORS INTO PAYING CUSTOMERS IN 7 STEPS

BY LLOYD IRVIN

THE MOST IMPORTANT MEASURE OF YOUR WEBSITE'S SUCCESS IS HOW MUCH MONEY IT MAKES YOU.

It doesn't matter how good your website looks or what it tells everyone about you.

The success of your site is determined by how many of the people who visit it actually become your customers.

You then have to do whatever is necessary to turn more of these visitors into customers, get them to stay with you longer and spend more money.

In order to do that, you need to follow a clearly defined process.

Here are the seven steps you need to follow to turn more of your website visitors into profitable customers.

STEP 1: FOCUS ON THE OPT-IN

When someone visits your website, they probably found it because they are interested in what you are offering—whether they found it via a search, as a result of your marketing or through a link or recommendation from someone else.

In a handful of cases, they will be ready right then to pick up the phone and call you or buy what you are offering.

But the reality is most visitors are likely to be interested in what you offer, but not ready to purchase right now.

If you let them just visit your site, the chances are they will never return—even if they are very interested in what you offer. So it's absolutely vital you do whatever you can to get their contact details so that you can follow up with them until they are ready to buy.

When you collect the information, you are creating a pool of people interested in what you offer and you can keep going back to them. This is the basis of what is called "two-step marketing."

The first step is to collect their information; the second is to keep following up with them until they buy.

In order to collect their details, you need a box on your site where they can enter their name and email so that you can follow up with them using an email autoresponder.

When someone gives you their details, this is called an opt-in.

For example, if 100 people visit your site and 60 of them join your list, your opt-in rate is 60%. One of your tasks is to keep making changes to get the opt-in rate as high as possible.

Here are five ways to get the best possible results from your opt-in box.

- **Make the opt-in very prominent:** The main opt-in box must be very easy to see. The best location is normally the top right of the page and it must be visible as soon as someone visits your site—no matter the size of their computer screen.

- **Use pop-ups and pop-unders:** You may hate them but pop-ups and pop-unders are very effective at increasing your opt-in rate. If someone is interested in what you offer, they will respond. You should use them when someone exits your site to make sure you capture as many visitors as possible.

- **Have multiple opt-in boxes:** Some people will scroll down past the main opt-in box so you must have multiple opt-in locations— top, middle and bottom of the page. You should also have them on every page, not just the home page.

- **Tell people exactly what to do:** Always state very clearly where people should enter their information and what they will get in return. Large arrows pointing to the opt-in box plus visuals and bold titles promoting the benefits can help greatly.

- **Test different options:** The less information you ask for, the more opt-ins you will get. For example, just asking for the email is better than asking for name and email—but if you don't get the name, you can't personalize the message. Asking for the phone number will reduce the number of opt-ins further but may enable you to follow up more effectively.

STEP 2: OFFER A GREAT WIDGET

To persuade people to give you their contact details, you need to offer something of value as a 'bribe' in exchange for those details. I call this a 'widget'. Your widget could be something like a free DVD, a free report/ guide, a free online video, a series of tips, etc. It has to be good enough to get them to give you their contact information. To get started, a poor widget is better than no widget; but the better your widget, the more names you will capture.

A better widget also gives them a more positive impression of what you can offer and makes people more likely to stay on your list.

Your widget has to be appropriate to what you offer and be relevant and valuable to your market.

There are several ways to create a widget easily:

- Create a short report with answers to the most common questions you are asked

- Produce a list of tips relevant to your market

- Hire a freelancer on a site, such as elance.com,
  to write a special report

- Have someone interview you and offer an mp3 of the interview

- Record a short video—or use one you have prepared
  for another purpose

To make your widget more effective, give it an appealing title using something like "7 Secrets" or "10 Tips" and have a graphic created to use on your site to attract attention.

It's a good idea to test different widgets, different titles and different wordings when promoting them to see what gets you the best results.

STEP 3: GET FULL CONTACT DETAILS

While asking for just the email address or name plus email address will get you higher response initially, it's usually a good idea to go on and get the full contact details – i.e. the home address and phone number.

These days you are lucky if 75% of your emails get through but, if you have a physical address and send a mailer, a postcard or a DVD, almost 100% of them get through.

You can get the full contact information by taking people to a second page after they have entered their name and email address. You then ask them to give you their full details on this page in exchange for a physical widget such as a DVD or CD.

Sending something physical to someone's house is 10 times more powerful than just sending an email as they have something they can hold in their hand. It may appear to cost more but, provided you know how much it costs you to make a sale and how much a potential customer is worth to you, it can be a wise investment. If you have a strong sales process, you can even call them up as soon as they enter their phone number.

With this two-stage approach, even if someone doesn't give you their full contact details, you still have their email from stage one and can follow up with the autoresponder messages.

STEP 4: FOLLOW UP IMMEDIATELY

The big mistake a lot of people make when collecting contact details is they seem to think collecting the details is enough.

The truth is that getting the contact details is just the start of the process—and the start of what you hope will be a very long relationship.

So you need to make sure you begin the process of establishing that relationship immediately. You need to help people get to know you quickly and discover what you can offer.

If you don't do this from the first day, they will have forgotten who you are within a week or two.

So get started right away telling your story and giving them valuable information.

The big advantage of using autoresponders is that you can have all these messages set up in advance so that they go out automatically. Once they are written, you can go on using them for years.

You may well be spending money on Yellow Pages, Google AdWords, radio, TV or whatever to generate the traffic that brought this person to your website.

Now you need to start working to make sure you get a return on that investment.

If you don't follow up right away, you are wasting the time and money you have invested in bringing them to your site and persuading them to sign up.

STEP 5: MAKE AN IRRESISTIBLE OFFER

When you start building the relationship, you want to demonstrate that you can deliver valuable information. You don't want to be in their face selling every moment.

It's just like building a relationship in your personal life. You don't normally suggest marriage the moment you meet someone you like.

That's usually the way to end the relationship before it even starts. If the people receiving your emails think you are in their face the whole time, they will quickly unsubscribe.

However, the problem many people have is that they go to the opposite extreme.

They may send out lots of emails but never actually make an offer or ask for the sale.

You are sending out emails because you want to build a profitable relationship. So your email sequence needs to include opportunities for them to deepen the relationship by buying something from you.

People are on your list because they are interested in what you can do for them, so they want to know how you can help.

The exact offer will depend on your product or service. It may be an invitation to make a small initial purchase; it may be the option to attend a webinar or they could make an appointment to visit you.

Whatever offer you plan to make, you need to make it clear, you need to make it as irresistible as possible and you need to specify exactly what you want people to do.

STEP 6: STAY IN TOUCH UNTIL THEY BUY OR DIE

The real key to success in turning website visitors into long-term customers is staying in touch with them until they are ready to buy.

People will develop their relationship with you at different paces.

Some people will want what you offer right away and will buy everything you present to them.

Others will happily continue receiving your emails until the moment is right for them and this may be quite a long time after they sign up.

I've had people staying on my lists for years before they buy anything from me but they then become great customers.

If somebody is no longer interested in what you have to say, they can unsubscribe from your list. People will do that and you should not worry about it. Focus your attention on the people who remain on your list. They are the potential customers.

You grow the relationship over time by continuing to send valuable information, whether in the form of regular emails, online newsletters or one-off mailings.

You want to follow up with them in as many ways as possible both by email and, wherever possible, offline through direct mail and postcards.

You should also maintain the relationship by building contact through other channels such as social media. You want to integrate your various strands of marketing activity as much as possible.

Different people prefer contact in different ways so you need to make contact in as many ways as possible.

The frequency of contact depends on your offer and your market. I am involved in niches where I email my lists every day. I also have others where the contact is less frequent.

You need to figure out what frequency works best for your market but you need to stay in touch.

STEP 7: CHECK, CHANGE AND CONTINUE IMPROVING

If you want to turn as many of your website visitors as possible into customers, you need to keep improving your results. For example, you should track which messages get the most clicks, which get the most people to call and which cause the most people to opt-out.

With good autoresponder services, you can track which individual people on your list are opening specific emails and which are not. Different people respond to different things so, when someone doesn't open your email, you can send them the same message a few days later with a different subject line.

Most people don't take time to segment their lists like that but you can improve your results significantly by doing this over and over.

You should always test different approaches as changes can make a big difference to the number of opt-ins.

For example, on one of my sites, I made a simple change to the sales copy above the opt-in box and the signups increased by more than 20%. A small increase in the number of opt-ins can potentially be worth a lot of money.

So testing everything from the wording on your opt-in form to the subject lines in your emails can help you make more money much faster.

GETTING THE BEST RESULTS

When someone visits your website, you have a few seconds in which to grab their attention and encourage them to give you their details.

You then need to follow the right process to build a relationship with them so that you turn them into paying customers who stay with you long-term.

When you follow the process effectively, you will end up not only with a very successful website. You will also have a highly profitable business.

ABOUT LLOYD

Lloyd Irvin is a member of that very small group of entrepreneurs who have built multi-million dollar businesses both offline and online.

He is also one of the few who devotes as much time to helping others succeed in business as he does to building his own.

His commitment to martial arts—he is a former Brazilian Jiu-Jitsu World champion—led to him setting up his own martial arts school. However, he struggled to make money at first and quickly recognized the need to change his approach.

Breaking the Mold

He broke the mold in martial arts by being one of the first to use direct marketing strategies to attract new students.

Despite initial criticism from others, his marketing success allowed him to quickly build one of the USA's leading martial arts academies.

Marketing campaigns delivering a steady stream of new students have led to his academy producing several world champions, UFC champions and a world champion kids team.

Creating Millionaires

In addition to building his own academy, he is passionate about showing other martial arts school owners how to change the way they work to easily attract more students and make more money.

With his help, many go from charging less than $100 a month to charging 5-figure fees while still getting more students.

His mastermind groups, coaching programs, live events and home study courses have helped hundreds of martial arts school owners around the world. As a result, many have turned their interest in martial arts from a virtual "hobby" into a million dollar business.

Million Dollar Days

Having mastered the techniques of direct marketing and internet marketing in building his school, Lloyd took this knowledge into a range of other markets.

Initially seeing internet marketing as a way of adding a few thousand dollars a month to his income, he realized the potential was much greater when his first online launch made over $180,000 in just one day.

Since then, he has built multi-million dollar businesses in many different markets including several million dollar product launches, with one making more than $1.7 million in just one day.

He has now built successful businesses in several niches including diet, healthcare and multi-level marketing.

His proven marketing strategies – backed by specialist teams he has built - enable him to use technology and marketing expertise to dominate the key markets where he operates and to enter new markets easily.

Keys to Success

As an enthusiastic fan of Napoleon Hill's "Think and Grow Rich", he attributes his success to being willing to master specialized skills such as direct marketing, internet marketing and copywriting.

He also believes in the importance of taking fast action and implementing what you learn if you want to get results.

Lloyd believes especially strongly in the power of the mastermind principle and having the right mentors. He feels it's vital to surround yourself with people who share your aspirations or who are already successful in fields where you want to get results.

Through combining a world champion mindset with consistently applying proven marketing strategies, Lloyd Irvin continues to build multi-million-dollar businesses and help others do the same.

www.MyMarketingSecrets.com

www.MMAMillionaires.com

CHAPTER 17

MARKET SMARTER, NOT HARDER

BY GUS KALOTI

E veryone wants their business to be more successful, from beginning businesspeople launching startups, to owners of underperforming businesses, to already successful business owners looking for explosive growth. In the work that I do, be it as president of Inovia Health, as a management consultant and success coach for dental practices, in traveling and media appearances, or in researching the books I write, I interact with many people and hear one question over and over again: "How can I be successful?" It's a complex question with many possible answers, however, in this era of a shifting economy and constantly evolving technology, a key area of focus to amplify success is in smarter marketing. Specifically, smart business owners must bridge the gap between the traditional marketing strategies that businesses have harnessed for years, partnering them with online marketing methods that are changing as fast as the technologies that support them. It sounds daunting, but it doesn't have to be. Like everything worthwhile, it it simply takes work—and a well-devised checklist.

175

Consider the example of a dental practice in New York City. This practice was underperforming to the point of being unviable. In my initial assessment of their strengths and weaknesses, I identified a massive opportunity. They had virtually no marketing, (a budget item that gets redlined by many businesses in survival mode). This was a huge problem, as reactionary survival modes often only hasten demise. My first advice was, "Market—get your name out there again, because you can't afford not to." Convinced, the client started by establishing an online presence. It used to be for dentists, like many other businesses, an ad in the Yellow Pages or a blanket mailing was enough. That's no longer the case in our networked world.

According to the Online Marketing Institute London, in their report "The State of Social Media 2012," one out of every seven minutes spent online is on Facebook. Social networks create new life for a business, and my client began updating a Facebook page daily with motivational quotes, images or videos, and basically any relevant / interesting content that demonstrated the business was still alive. People started paying attention again. As the likes grew, the credibility of the practice did too, because potential customers evaluate your business based on your online presence. The more followers you have on social accounts, the more credibility you demonstrate.

We were increasing interest for the struggling practice, but we needed to get patients in the door. I knew a blockbuster promotion was something this practice needed. Studying the potentials, I determined that a popular, invisible braces product would resonate well. We took a multi-prong approach. We ran a Facebook test promotion, and when we saw we were on the right track by the response, we took advantage of a traditional marketing tool, a direct mail campaign. Armed with targeted demographics, we got our message in front of potential patients, and then I advised, "Now get them online." That's the key to bridging the gap—touching each customer on and offline. From the above referenced report, by 2015, 75% of ads will be socially enabled. Now is the time to embrace this technology. The print mailing got people's attention, it pointed them to the client's online presence, which demonstrated their popularity and credibility, passively building trust from the first impression. Because they were interested and felt comfortable, these new patients began booking. The practice continued what it was already doing well, giving great care, phenomenal service and value. Doing this, they converted the new patients into repeats. That's the way to grow a business. With a smart strategy, connecting traditional marketing and online marketing, this NYC practice went from barely surviving to being one of the largest invisible braces providers on the East coast, which was a miraculous recovery. That's how one established business, a dentists' office, turned their business around with the right marketing. Another question I'm asked constantly is: "How can I make my new product launch successful?" My advice is clear-cut.

Bridging the gap between print and online marketing is crucial from the start. The example that leaps to mind is of a product I created, Smiles Plus, a dental discount program I pioneered in the Midwest that became the most successful and oft-duplicated of its kind in the region. Like most great ideas, it started with a personal passion. I believe people should have access to quality, affordable dental care. Too many people neglect their health because of a lack of insurance. The Smiles Plus program allowed individuals to buy a plan that would offer them contracted rates on dental services. Similar to what insured patients pay, but the rates negotiated by the dentists and Smiles Plus, bypassing inefficient insurance companies completely. We marketed this program offline at first, and it gained traction. People absorb information differently, so we covered multiple mediums, with print ads, as well as radio ads for those more auditory in their acquisition of information. Video is great for this, combining sight and sound. As a bridge, the same commercial you use for television can be a YouTube spot, linked to your Facebook page, or used on your website. Video is a marketing must.

At the same time we marketed offline, we established an online presence, and when it came time, we took our message digital. When people came to investigate Smiles Plus online, they saw a company with a thriving face in the networked world, helping them feel comfortable to become customers. We built trust, which is essential when making potential customers your customers for life. We thought creatively, rewarding our customers and extending our reach simultaneously. Existing customers providing referrals for new ones earned credit to spend on their own treatments, and "likes" on Facebook earned them extra credit. In the same promotion we used both word of mouth, the most traditional and vital of all marketing techniques; and we extended it online, by getting people online to learn more and follow the business. These followers built our credibility further—a cycle of success.

As word spread about Smiles Plus, and potential customers found us online, we gained customers far from the region the program was offered, and many drove hours or even flew in to use our dentists. The testimonials we got from those very satisfied customers made acquiring new customers easier still. When you offer a great product, satisfy customers, get the word out, and you are consistent, success follows. Smiles Plus has been a tremendous success that I'm proud of, not only because it was profitable, but because it helped people that might not have otherwise had access to dental care. From these two examples of how marketing saved a failing dental practice and grew it into a valuable one, and from the successful launch of a product using the power of offline and online marketing synergistically, how can individuals and businesses apply these lessons to find more success? The following "List of Six" are principles that any individual or business can use to market better, bridge the gap between print and online marketing, and to be more successful.

LIST OF SIX

1. **Run Your Business "Inside Out":** Consumers don't solely purchase with their wallets—they use their hearts and brains, seeking distinctive brands with character at their center. As a businessperson, start by looking at who you are, your inner core. Take those passions and values and use them for the basis of starting and running your business, and use them to set the course for your marketing efforts. Run your business as a leader, the same way you live your life. Successful marketing starts with a great thing to market, and *market what's inside you*. By working from the "inside out" your authenticity will set you apart every time, allowing you to be great at what you do.

2. **Tell People:** You have a great business, a business you can be excited about, and you need customers. The best way to get them is by telling them who you are, what you do, how you're going to satisfy their needs, and the value you offer. Tell people this every way you can. Be smart about it, know when to cast a wide net and when to target focus, and do it. Establish a presence

online through a website and social media because this is no longer optional, its part of the purchasing process for today's consumers. Build the credible web presence and take your message offline as well. Send targeted mailings, like I did with the NYC dentist mentioned above, but with that printed message get your potential customer online, too. Broadcast the message, bridge the gap and the customers will come.

3. **Show People:** People want to know your business, what you are and what you do. Show them. This starts before a client ever walks into your establishment. Quality marketing materials communicate professionalism. A well-done video on your website or Facebook can begin to forge the relationship that has to be built to establish lasting customers. The same video can be used as a DVD you send to new clients. Let them get to know you, because *you* are what they're buying. When they become clients, continue to show them. Providing great service isn't just good business, it also reinforces your marketing message and extends it: the service they receive is an invitation for repeat business.

4. **Be Consistent:** Consistency is applied several ways; in branding, in business practice, and in marketing efforts. When you are branding yourself, be consistent. For example, a high-end business that worked hard to develop a luxury reputation shouldn't suddenly be a discounter. Business practices need to similarly follow through. If a customer comes to you with the expectation you've branded, and their expectations aren't met, they won't repeat the mistake. Experience must match expectations for optimal customer reactions. Finally, in your marketing efforts, consistency pays. State your message and demonstrate it thoughtfully and steadily. Give your efforts time and the attention they need to work. Be proactive in the research that precedes launching a marketing campaign; don't only be reactive when an ill-planned effort yields poor results. Proactive businesses make more money than reactive ones. Inconsistency undermines marketing efforts, and undermines businesses.

5. **Be Credible:** People don't buy from, or use the services from, the untrustworthy. When you work from the inside out, with your core values influencing all you do, you are already running your

business authentically and therefore credibility doesn't need to be generated—just demonstrated and reinforced. One great source of credibility comes from a positive word-of-mouth reputation. Give people a reason to spread the word about your business, such a consumer credit for customer referrals like we used with the Smiles Plus Program. This kind of marketing goes a long way, both online and offline. Credible businesses need a web presence that illustrates their worth. Spend the time and effort to develop a useful and informative website, and social media accounts that are engaging, well-maintained and followed. This will help your business demonstrate that you are an authority at what you do, and that customers can trust you. If your clients trust you, they'll stick with you, and that makes businesses less vulnerable to economic downturns and other threats. Credible businesses are lasting ones.

6. **Adjust as Needed:** The last concept on the List of Six is certainly not least. When marketing your business, you do the research, make a plan, execute it well, and track the results. Then what?

Learn from what you've done and adjust. Online marketing efforts can be tracked with increasingly sophisticated analytics, giving your business better than ever insight into your customers. If marketing campaigns don't deliver the intended results, take the time to learn why they didn't work. The issue could be that you haven't yet found the right formula for your individual business to balance online and offline marketing. When a campaign is successful, take the time to understand what you did right, then replicate and improve upon it in future marketing efforts. "We can always market better," I tell my many clients. This post-assessment and adjustment builds future and lasting success, which is the intention behind all marketing efforts. To get more hands-on and various insight into my marketing techniques, <u>guskaloti.com</u> should be your next stop, where you gain valuable information, coaching, management tips, and much more. "I am sure you care about your success as much as I do."

ABOUT GUS

Author and president of Inovia Healthcare, Gus Kaloti redefined dental practice success, smashing old barriers to maximize efficiency and skyrocket profitability. Kaloti's entrepreneurial and industry-specific experience turns around underperforming practices and delivers quantifiable results with his proven combination of sound management, penetrative marketing, and emerging technology-based solutions. He is set to be featured in *USA Today*, *The Wall Street Journal*, and on ABC, NBC, CBS and FOX. His skilled dental coaching develops your team, increases your reach, grows your practice, and gives back what Kaloti realizes is most valuable: your time.-- Gus Kaloti, Leader in Innovation

CHAPTER 18

LEVERAGING TIME AND RESOURCES:

HOW FARMING THE RIGHT LEADS WILL CHANGE YOUR BUSINESS

BY GORDON DEY

A good day for an average Realtor would probably flow something like this: send a few emails to prospective clients, make some phone calls to potential clients, get one or two on the phone, get rejected by most of the prospects you actually made contact with, spend hours preparing a presentation for a prospect, meet with prospect, get a listing. If that Realtor is statistically blessed, his listing will sell within a couple of months. In a perfect world, one presentation equals one sale, but it is not a perfect world is it? Moreover, who really wants to be "average"?

A niche that allows a Realtor to leverage his time and resources changes the game. Why settle for a single when you can get a triple or even a homerun? While a typical Realtor markets to owners and buyers, "typical" leads to "average" results. Any Realtor can change the 1 to

183

1 ratio of transactions to sales to one transaction equals 100 sales by simply following a few key steps past owners and buyers only know: getting to new homebuilders.

The beauty of my system is that the initial process resembles any other lead farming that Realtors or other business people normally go through. You generate your lead list, set up constant contact with the leads in a follow-up system, and convert those contacts into sales; however, you leverage your time and resources to achieve greater results. Farming leads really does resemble traditional farming of a field. You scatter seeds and after much care, they will flourish. However, as any real farmer knows, the quality of the field you have prepared will directly affect your crop—it will determine if you reap abundantly or sparsely for the same effort.

For the purpose of this chapter, I will show you how farming the new homebuilder market can dramatically change your annual yield. Even if you are not in Real Estate, you can apply these ideas to your business by simply selecting a niche market that will bear fruit more abundantly than the leads you have sowed before.

WHO IS YOUR TARGET?

Homebuilders are investors who put their hard-earned money into business to make more money. An investor with $1 million invested in four homes *does not make a dime if those homes do not sell*. If he sells those four homes this year, his return on investment might hit his mark. However, help this same builder sell the first four homes in the first half of the year so that he can build and sell four more in the second half of the year, and YOU just helped him double his profit. Your goal as the Realtor advisor to a new homebuilder is to help him sell as many cycles of building four homes and returning his initial investment plus profit as possible, which then can be used to build four more homes in the same year. When you increase his ROI, you become a member of his very important cabinet and become indispensable.

Knowing the goals and needs of your farm area changes your status from sales person to advisor. If you are not an expert yet, or have few transactions under your belt, find the National Association of Expert Advisors. Members' goal is to teach, share, mentor, and lead. Get yourself an expert to assist you in building your knowledge base, and then, your customer base.

WHAT IS IN IT FOR YOU?

If the average Realtor only sells six to eight homes per year, and invests about $150 per month on average in marketing his business, that Realtor is never reaching his full potential. What tends to happen in a Real Estate office is there are a few top producers and the rest stand around drinking coffee. Do you want to be a top producer? If yes, consider this. Think of the number of hours you normally spend preparing for a client. You could spend 1-2 hours weekly for each property you sell just for the listing presentation alone. Add to that your three-hour preparation time for a total of five hours of research, preparation and meeting time, and the risk that this prep time will yield you nothing. Conversely, when you meet with and sign a New Homebuilder, your initial listing presentation with the builder happens *once* to net, say, 20 different sales! That is about a five-hour investment for sales that if pursued individually would have taken about 100 hours of your time.

PURSUE

How do you farm New Home Builders?

Establish New Home Builders as a target of your business. Get lists of the New Home Builders in your area from the Home Builders' Association. When you become a member of the HBA, you get access to these valuable lists. You also are invited to their events. Before you groan and say that you cannot stand to go to those functions, you should be aware that Meet & Greets serve you for two reasons. First, you have been *invited* to attend. Prospects are more likely to talk with you in a meaningful way when they meet you at an event than they would if you cold-called their office. Second, everyone who attends a Meet & Greet type of event is there to meet people. Approach your prospects, give them your 15-20 second elevator speech, and then ask them "How can I help you?"

Spend time getting to know how to help them. Make your efforts more about them and less about you. Builders are in need of assistance because they are competing with short sales and distress sales, and foreclosures.

PRESENT

Once you have a rapport with the builder, it is time to get in front of them for a presentation. Getting to the presentation will require diligence: follow up with email or, even better, a short handwritten note that says, "It was great to meet you at the HBA social." Put them into your personal follow-up rotation. Once you have been in front of your lead before, as at the social functions, it is far easier to get in front of your contact again.

Please remember that your goal remains to get in front of them again. Email is nice and quick, but it should not be your first choice for a first contact with your contacts, ever. Keep your eye on the prize. You want to be in front of these people at least once a month until they recognize that they need you. When you finally get the opportunity to make your presentation to them in person, you don't want to blow it. New Home Builders are smart business people. Be prepared to offer them concrete financial reasons why it makes sense to do business with you.

DEMONSTRATE VALUE

Your value to them is complete outsourcing of their sales department to you. You offer him professional sales that he does not need to train, manage, or market to get results. You will want to show the homebuilders that you are saving them money at every turn. The builder pays the same commission compensation he would if it was his sales force plus the builders' split with an outside buyer's agent; however, you cover all his sales force expenses and you save him money on any advertising, training, time to manage sales force and his headaches will be gone. Instead of his investing hours in market research, you are Johnny on the Spot with the right numbers at your fingertips to be his trusted business advisor!

Two key facts to have at the ready for your homebuilder prospect are Absorption Rate and Market Share. The absorption rate for your area can save the homebuilder money in two ways: this data tells him how many homes like his sold last year and for how much they sold in the areas he wants to build. If your builder has plans to build 20 houses at a particular price point and square footage, but only nine such homes sold in the area last year, he could be waiting a while for a return on his investment unless he competitively prices his homes. Every new homebuilder will know that his market share affects his bottom line. Consult with him to find out what his pricing threshold is in order to increase his market share. Show him that by pricing his homes competitively he will sell more houses more quickly, thus freeing his money to be reinvested that much sooner.

ASK FOR THE BUSINESS

"Do you feel that having my experience and expertise would save you money?" should be your next question after your presentation. If the answer is still "No" and your prospect is still not ready, put him back on your follow up list. Send a thank you note for your visit. Reiterate in your note that you can save him money, time, and hassles.

PROCESS

If you asked for the business and got the initial appointment with one of your targets from your farm list, it is time to do your homework. Prepare all the relevant numbers for the homebuilder with whom you will be meeting. At this point, unless you are an experienced sales person or Realtor, you want to enlist the help of a power agent. If you do not know one of these top producers yourself, you can go to the MLS to find an agent in your office who has sold many properties. You want the one who really sells as a career and not on a part-time basis. This agent can assist you to polish your presentation and be ready for your appointment.

After you earn their listing(s), your process reverts to what you already know; it follows the same marketing process:

Create internet presence: 90% of all buyers are coming to the internet.

- Track internet buyers

- Generate buyer interest

- Sell their properties

Obviously, getting to yes with one client from your farm list does not mean you stop farming. Farming is all about numbers. With builders you are probably going to hit about 1% of what you farm, but that average is still exceptional compared with the less than 1% return of direct mail. Farming the New Homebuilder market and achieving your 1% annual return, your business will be on fire. The equation for your six figure income simple + basic + success = repeat business. The five homes that the builder initially had to sell will quickly turn to 15 homes if you are doing your job well. Nevertheless, you will continue to farm your list and attend functions of the HBA. You will continue to seek out your prospects on a monthly basis until you get to yes.

BEYOND REAL ESTATE LEAD FARMING

As I mentioned before, you can apply this simple formula to almost any business. You need to locate the niche markets that have the greatest propensity for repeat business or multiple sales with repeat business. If you are direct marketing any product, to who can you market and have built-in repeat business? Just as with real estate, knowing your market and the data of your industry will give you a leg up above the crowd. Is there an association you can join where you will meet potential customers such as a chamber of commerce or local clubs or organizations? Again, your goal is to be invited to events where you can meet your prospects in a setting that is conducive to conversation and where people congregate specifically to meet others in their industry.

Few people strive to be "average," or worse, mediocre. Don't settle for selling the average 6-8 houses a year that keeps other agents happy. If all things were equal, would you really settle for one-fifth of what you would earn if you only followed this simple plan to a six-figure income? Leverage your time to your best advantage. In the words of William Penn, "time is what we want most, but…what we use worst." Make every at-bat a homerun; let the average people be happy with a single.

ABOUT GORDON

Gordon Dey is a best-selling author and marketing expert who is regularly sought out by the new homebuilders for his opinions on market conditions and marketing campaigns that really work. Gordon has been seen on NBC, CBS, ABC, and FOX affiliates. Gordon is known for his innovative marketing skills that produce results. Gordon was recognized as the No. 1 Broker/Owner in the State of Florida by a large real estate franchise for having the highest average agent productivity in sales volume and transactions sold. Gordon's ability to attract New Home Builders to list with him or his company was a huge part of his success.

Focusing on New Homebuilders was a game changer for Gordon. Gordon and his team have sold over 400 new homes. Gordon has helped even his newest agent list new homebuilders and begin to enjoy this profitable real estate niche market.

To learn more about Gordon Dey and how you can receive the Free Special Report "Working with New Home Builders" visit www.GordonDeyNewHomes.com or call him at (850) 748-0575.

www.GordonDeyNewHomes.com

CHAPTER 19

HOW TO BUILD A MOBILE WEBSITE THAT CONVERTS VISITORS TO CLIENTS...

THE TOP 9 STRATEGIES REVEALED

BY GUS SKARLIS

DID YOU KNOW THAT...

- **92% Of ALL Local Searches Were Done On A Mobile Device?**

- **86% Are Looking For Phone, Contact & Address Information?**

- **50% Will NOT Return To A Site That Is Not Mobile Optimized?**

- **40% Have Went To A Competitor Site That WAS Mobile Optimized?**

- **35% Of All Your Current Website Traffic Is Coming From Mobile Devices?**

In fact, by 2013, there will be more searches done on mobile devices than desktop devices. Here's a brief introduction to mobile websites.

WHAT IS A MOBILE WEBSITE?

The simple answer is… a website that will display correctly on a mobile device.

In order to achieve a website that will render on these smaller screens, a new set of code and standards has been developed that is totally different from the code your "desktop" website was built on.

This new code platform is called **HTML 5** and **CSS 3** and this will allow your pages to load much quicker and also be indexed in the new mobile search engines.

The reason you should build a mobile website is because <u>your desktop website was built for a 15-inch or larger screen sizes and most mobile devices are around 3 inches.</u>

See how this can present a problem for visitors trying to navigate your website on a mobile device?

MOBILE WEBSITE TIP:

The search engines have stated that any website that does not have mobile compatible code

(HTML5 & CSS 3) will not be listed in their indexes.

RESOURCE: Find out if your website has mobile compatible code:
http://www.MobileWebsiteTester.com

RULE #1: INTENT TO TAKE ACTION

This is going to come as a surprise, but your current website content is basically worthless on a mobile device because mobile visitors want quick information and answers.

You need to build your mobile website so it allows the mobile visitor to take fast action. But first, you need to figure out what action you'd like them to take...

- Do you want their email address?

- Do you want them to call you?

- Do you want to capture their phone number?

- Do you want them to buy something?

- Do you want them to watch a video?

Remember, your mobile visitors are on the go, at the mall, in between the kids' lessons and practice—so build your mobile website with this in mind.

MOBILE WEBSITE TIP:

Make it easy for your mobile visitors to take action.

RULE #2: BEST MOBILE DESIGNS

When it comes to designing a mobile website, everyone has an opinion—but if you stick to these

3 types of mobile layouts you'll build a winner.

Horizontal Layouts: These layouts are best for e-commerce sites that have multiple categories and sub-categories. They are clean and easy to use for visitors.

Button Layouts: This style looks like an app because it will generally have 9 buttons (3 rows of 3) with icons. Visitors like these types of sites because they familiar with them and can easily identify the icon with the page content.

We have designed a lot of mobile websites but it seems the ones that get the best response are the **Image Layouts.**

What we do is take an image (or video) and overlay the navigation on top of the image. This creates a "stop in your tracks" mobile website that gets a lot of "oooohhs" and "aahhs."

MOBILE WEBSITE TIP:

Design a mobile website that screams "stop and look at me" because you only have a few seconds to capture their attention and interest.

RESOURCE: You can see examples of hundreds of different types of layouts at **http://www.MobileWebsites.com**

RULE #3: NAVIGATION

One of the most important secrets that gets higher conversions is to create a **Take Action**—which means we order the navigation pages from least resistance to highest resistance.

A sample mobile website navigation for a tanning salon would be:

- Watch Video
- About Us
- Download Free Report
- Call Us
- Buy Session
- Directions

This allows the visitor to follow a natural path of learning and exploring and lets them go directly to **an action page** without having to search your site.

MOBILE WEBSITE TIP:

The order of your navigation is just as important as the content so make sure all of your top level navigation has "take action."

RULE #4: TOP CONVERTING COLORS

Color makes no difference... the color you choose for your mobile website comes down to personal preference—**just don't do black!**

If you website is about the environment, green would be a good choice, if it has to do with babies then pink or blue would work fine.

Select your color theme with what a mobile visitor would expect as it will create instant identification. The last thing you want is to make your visitor guess what your site is about.

MOBILE WEBSITE TIP:

Most phones are black so be careful using a black background as this will make it very hard to read and navigate in low light settings.

RULE #5: MOBILE MARKETING

Mobile Marketing covers many different types of campaigns, but here are the only ones you need to be concerned with...

1. Text message marketing
2. Email marketing
3. Click To Call
4. QR Codes
5. Pay Per Click

Text message marketing is growing at a rapid pace and will soon be the most used form of marketing to visitors and clients.

Text messaging allows you send short messages directly to a person's mobile phone and over 98% of all text messages are opened by the recipient.

Here's how to do it: set up a one-line form on your mobile website with an offer for coupons, giveaways, alerts, appointments, events, discounts or newsletters.

When someone types in their phone number it will automatically send a text message back to them with your message... and now you can continue to send them messages for just a few pennies.

MOBILE WEBSITE TIP:

Don't use short codes—they are a waste of money. If you set up your mobile website correctly you do not need them.

EMAIL MARKETING:

75% of people say that they check email from their mobile device and this can present some problems.

You need to assume that your emails are being read on mobile devices and take the appropriate steps to ensure that your email content is mobile optimized as well as the click-through URL's.

MOBILE WEBSITE TIP:

Keep your emails short, preferably text and if you are requesting them to click-through make sure you are sending them to a mobile optimized page, video or form.

CLICK TO CALL:

With the advances in technology you can now "tap" on a phone number and it will automatically connect you with the number.

Make sure you add a click to call number on your mobile website so your visitors can easily connect with you.

Most developers add the click to call as a button that says "Click Here To Talk To Us" or something similar... but do not do this.

MOBILE WEBSITE TIP:

Make sure your 'click to call' is text with the phone number visible. This will help your search engine rankings and allow your visitors to read your phone number if they need to write it down.

QR CODES:

QR codes are those square bar codes you have probably seen in magazines, billboards or newspapers.

Here's how they work... a smartphone user takes a picture of the QR code and then are re-directed to:

- Mobile Website
- Facebook Page
- Phone Number
- LinkedIn Profile
- Twitter Profile
- YouTube Video
- Or just about any other "address" you want to send the visitor to.

They allow you take a long URL and embed it in an image that smart phones can scan.

Try It: Take a picture of this QR code to see how it works:
(make sure you have a QR code reader installed)
They are available for free at http://itunes.com or http://play.google.com

QR codes are great for marketing and you should put QR codes on your business cards, flyers, invoices and any printed material.

MOBILE WEBSITE TIP:
Do not use the free QR code generators found on the internet because if they shut down your QR codes will not work.

RULE #6: MOBILE SEARCH ENGINE OPTIMIZATION

The search engines now have a new mobile search engine that will only allow sites that are mobile compatible to be found:

Here's what you need to know...

```
Once Googlebot-Mobile crawls your URLs, we
then check for whether the URL is viewable
on a mobile device. Pages we determine aren't
viewable on a mobile phone won't be included
in our mobile site index (although they may
be included in the regular web index.
If it's not in a compatible format, the page
is ineligible for the mobile search index.
```

As you build your mobile website you will need to optimize your mobile website, just like you did with your desktop website.

*   Keywords
*   Title Tags
*   Meta Descriptions
*   Image Alt Tags
*   Micro Data
*   Mobile Site Maps

The most important part of mobile SEO is that you spend the time to set up the proper keywords and find the "buyer keywords"—buy, review, find, how to, who is, best and top.

Don't worry about the lower search numbers because these keywords show "intent" and these visitors will convert at a higher rate.

MOBILE WEBSITE TIP:

Submitting site maps is a secret of the top webmasters. In fact, the search engines have a new mobile sitemap that is just for your mobile content but you'll also need to submit all 4 sitemaps: Content, Mobile, Images and Video to Google, Yahoo, and Bing via their webmaster tools.

RESOURCE: Learn how micro data will get your mobile site ranked higher: **http://schema.org/docs/gs.html**

RULE #7: MOBILE WEBSITE VS. A MOBILE APP

There are a lot of theories about which to build and what is best for your business. Here's what I think:

1. Everyone should have a mobile website.
2. Mobile Apps are for larger companies like Paypal and Zynga.
3. Apps are more for games and tools.

While apps are cool, neat and fun, unless you have a specific reason to build one I believe you should build out your mobile website first and then build out an app to complement the website at a later date.

You must consider your market, clients and visitors. For example, a local chiropractor wanted to build a mobile app, but then we put the app use in a scenario.

The chiropractor would have to build the app for 3 platforms, market the app to their visitors and then have them go download the app versus just having a mobile website where they can quickly and easily find directions and phone number.

> ## MOBILE WEBSITE TIP:
> Right now 30% of your traffic is coming from mobile devices.
> Optimize your website first!

RULE #8: MOBILE PROFIT CENTERS

There are hundreds of additional ways that you can generate profits and sales from your mobile website. Here are a few examples...

- **Sell Gift Cards**: this works great for restaurants

- **Offer Memberships:** Chiropractors love this

- **Sell Complimentary Products & Kits:** Great for affiliate marketing

- **Thank You Page:** Put on an offer or affiliate link on your mobile thank you page

- **Autoresponders**: Capture and then follow up with email marketing

- **SMS Text Message Marketing:** capture phone numbers and then send out coupons or deals

- **Directory Listings:** Offer a premium listing or paid advertising

- **Members Only Area:** Allow your clients access to members only content

- **Advertising:** Show mobile ads on your mobile website

- **CPA/Affiliate Offers**: Create a mobile blog with CPA or affiliate offers

---

MOBILE WEBSITE TIP:

When you build your mobile website make sure you can sell products or services from it. Even if you don't have mobile e-commerce plans right now make sure it is available because there are huge opportunities for ANY WEBSITE to make money from mobile e-commerce.

RULE #9: MISTAKES TO AVOID

1. **Ask this question** before you hire any mobile website developer:

   "How Will I Manage The Mobile Website?"

   The reason that you need to ask this question is to make sure the developer has a mobile platform. The last thing you want is to have them build a mobile site that you can not easily manage or access.

2. **Don't over-think the design**. As long as you build with "Intent To Take Action" the design is secondary. You will not get a visitor to take action because of a "cool" website.

3. **Automated 1 Click mobile website builders don't work...** There are just too many variables, code and languages to build you an optimized mobile website. They can do some of the work but not all.

In addition, these companies built software to take the place of staff so they rarely offer any support or help after the sale.

4. **Call and email the developer before you build.** Make sure they have a business license, HTML5, CSS 3 developer credentials and are writing their own code.

5. **Find out about their redirection code.** Most will use a subdomain of their website domain. <u>Make sure you can use m.yourdomain.com.</u> If you can't use your own subdomain do not build with them.

6. **You get what you pay for.** If you want to spend $10 per month then you are going to get a $10 mobile website.

7. **Check to see if they have an apple developer license.** If they have built a mobile website I can almost guarantee they have built an app.

8. **What about Tablet content?** Find out how they display content to tablet users. If they show your desktop site to tablet users **it will not be optimized**—if they show your mobile site to tablet users it will be under-optimized.

9. **How do they handle changes, updates and modifications?** Do they charge per incident, per hour? Who do you contact? What is the process? Know the answers to these questions.

ABOUT GUS

Gus Skarlis is a mobile website and online marketing expert who has spent the past 8 years developing thousands of websites with first page results.

Because of his expert status in the technology world, Gus is regarded as the "Go-To Guy" for companies and small businesses looking to build, market and manage their mobile website.

Frustrated with constantly trying to implement the myriad of 3rd party software and code into his websites, he founded MobileWebsites.com in 2009, a company that provides the only mobile platform that will manage your mobile content, SEO and marketing from 1 area **without having to deal with multiple vendors and software products.**

To learn more about Gus Skarlis and mobile websites watch the video "The Shocking Truth About Mobile Websites" at
http://www.MobileWebsites.com or call Toll-Free **1-800-660-9395**

CHAPTER 20

21ST CENTURY MARKETING AND ANALYTICS:

THE SCIENCE BEHIND MARKETING MIRACLES

BY JAMES WALKER

L et's say you have a thousand dollars you've budgeted to gamble in Las Vegas. And you have to determine where that money's going to give you the biggest pay-off. Are you going to hit the poker tables at Caesars, the blackjack tables at Bellagio or just try the slots at the Golden Nugget?

Now, you could just randomly try each of those casinos and/or each of those games. Or, let's say you had some inside information—and you had the exact odds of each game at each casino. Let's go further and say you had a software program that could tell you the exact amount of your money to bet on which game at which casino to have the best odds of a big pay-off.

You'd probably let that program tell you what to do, because the numbers don't lie. And you want the odds on your side.

Well, Marketing Analytics isn't much different than that process. With Marketing Analytics, you can determine where you should place your marketing "bets." When you're ready to roll out your new product, service or just want to sell your brand in a high-profile way, Marketing Analytics gives you the best shot at reaching a receptive audience with a track record of spending money on whatever it is you're selling.

If you're not putting Marketing Analytics to work for your business in this day and age, be warned—you're missing out on a real Marketing Miracle.

THE ANALYTICS REVOLUTION

In the past, Marketing Analytics were used to support whatever the main marketing message happened to be. In most cases, that message was concocted without the benefit of those analytics; no one gave them a thought as to being a creative force of their own. No, analytics were strictly a numbers game employed to make sure the campaigns developed by advertising gurus unrolled in as effective a manner as possible. To be fair, analytic systems were fairly primitive until recently.

Today, however, Marketing Analytics are a whole new ballgame. The combination of amazing new analytical techniques, amped-up computer power and instantaneous online resources has resulted in incredibly powerful software tools that have changed the marketing game forever. So powerful, in fact, that analytics are no longer there just to lend support. Instead, robust simulations can unlock dynamic opportunities that provide their own creative firepower—which drives new strategies and opens up game-changing marketing possibilities never before imagined.

At our international brand and marketing consultancy company, Prophet, we supply sophisticated marketing models for our clients everyday—which leads them to marketing decisions that avoid shot-in-the-dark guesswork and, instead, embrace solid results.

Let's look at four key areas where Marketing Analytics are really making a difference.

#1:   MARKETING MIX MODELING

No pilot sits in a real aircraft cockpit without first spending a certain amount of hours training in a flight simulator. Similarly, with our Marketing Mix Modeling analytics and software tools, we can simulate all the brands in a single category, in one ecosystem model, and decide on how to optimize the marketing mix; how much should be spent on advertising, promotions, and other marketing techniques.

With these tools, we can play an almost-infinite number of "what-if" games. For example, an expert modeling system, such as our Prophet-Modeler, can explore thousands of possible models to examine the historical impact of each marketing channel by region and other variables. We can also drill deeper and generate continual response curves for each media, each product, each product and so forth.

Another marketing mix optimization tool such as our Prophet-Allocator looks at multiple scenarios that reflect different investment levels in different areas. With this software, it's easy to see how one marketing investment feeds into another and creates a powerful synergy that adds up to more than the sum of its parts.

Live data visualizations are also now a reality as part of our client service. That means not relying on PowerPoints created weeks or months ago for data reference—it means accessing the latest information instantaneously so there's no question we're all dealing with the reality of today's 24/7 market.

#2:   CUSTOMER ANALYTICS

Of course, it's not enough to just take a look at *where* you can invest your marketing dollars; it's also critical to know *who* your best potential customers are and what their buying behavior is.

We believe that's a three-step process, beginning with **Customer Diagnostics**. What are your current customers' behavioral patterns of engagement over time? Using advanced analytics and simple metrics (such as overall amount spent by each customer or number of transactions over time), you can key in on such critical components as a customer's average lifetime value and the strength of their ongoing brand loyalty.

From that phase, we move into **Opportunity Identification and Prioritization**. You've already identified engagement patterns; now you can grow your understanding of what makes your customers tick and uncover their attitudes and motivations; category behavior with your brand as well as your competitors'; transactional and service behavior; and their typical response to marketing efforts.

Marketing Analytics can take this information and determine just what elements can improve customer engagement and sales conversions. This, in turn, can be the "inspiration" for a marketing campaign that hits all the right buttons in the most effective way - in order to create the best possible ROI from your marketing efforts.

The final phase of Customer Analytics is, of course **Activation**, or putting all this data to work so you can begin to realize results. The previous phase undoubtedly uncovered some "low-hanging fruit" that will be easy to take advantage of; but more complex marketing concepts will undoubtedly also need to be evaluated. By using efficient "test and learn" plants, these ideas can be fine-tuned and prioritized to see which are the most effective.

How do Customer Analytics work in reality? Well, we had one client, a digital photo services provider, that needed to improve customer engagement. Our data shattered some of their long-held beliefs, such as that the bulk of their customer base only bought from them during the holidays, since revenues spiked in that time period. It turned out these holiday shoppers only represented *seven percent* of the total customer base—which meant a huge opportunity was being ignored for year-round business.

Ultimately, the company put together marketing and customer service data for the first time to truly understand their customer engagement. The result? A thirty-five percent *reduction* in marketing campaign investments and a ten percent *increase* in annual revenues.

That's what ROI is all about.

#3: PRICE, PROMOTION AND SKU ANALYTICS

Pricing is not one of the sexiest aspects of marketing, but it is one of the most critical. Obviously, the margins a business makes as a result of its pricing enables it to grow or causes it financial pain.

But we firmly believe that it's wrong to focus on price alone. Assortment (SKU groupings), promotions and pricing are all "joined at the hip" and have to be integrated into any Marketing Analytics. All three must work together to achieve maximum results.

Most companies only correlate sales and pricing with a possible inclusion of promotions; more often than not, SKU offerings aren't considered. When they are, however, the difference is profound. Proctor & Gamble is one company that is renowned for its analytics in this area. They conquered the disposable razor category with its Gillette brand, even though that category was formerly crowded with products from Bic and Schick, thanks to Gillette's "ladder" of tiered products, including their Turbo, Fusion and ProGlide sub-brands.

To begin the Market Analytics of price, SKU offering and promotion, you have to engage in the following key activities:

- Understand your target consumers

- Identify potential selling channel alternatives

- Evaluate the consumer/occasion fit

- Evaluate the brand and partner fit

- Prioritize and select the most attractive channels

From there, you can address various pricing strategies as they pertain to such issues as customer management, product life cycle, operational issues, bundling and upselling and synergistic opportunities. In the next phase, you can build and test various scenarios designed to exploit identified pricing opportunities and create pricing plans to put into action.

A disciplined pricing strategy, linked to a brand strategy, creates the conditions for meeting short-term financial targets while building a vibrant and robust long-term brand. This can be accomplishing by using the enormous power of cutting-edge Marketing Analytics to optimize SKU and pricing for maximum commercial impact.

#4:   CHANNEL AND SALES FORCE OPTIMIZATION

Marketing Analytics gives us many major advantages out in the field as well, where the actual selling gets done. New techniques and software, as well as data feeds from sales force automation tools, allow us to develop optimized channel strategies, the best messaging to different customers, and the capability to design the ideal sales force. That sales force should employ the right mix of different types of reps allocating their time to different customers in different territories in the most efficient and effective way possible.

But, first, let's talk about channels. Channels are vital to the brand experience and cannot be ignored. For example, you can buy Ralph Lauren products online, in its directly-owned stores, at outlet locations or at a department store. Each channel has its own unique pricing considerations. Is there more value (i.e. a higher price) to a shopper in a Ralph Lauren store rather than a department store such as a Macy's or Nordstrom's? Solid channel analytics will provide the answer.

What every company wants is a sales force that's optimized for the most profit and the most impact. That process begins by defining the basic metrics of the sales force, including:

- The number of different audiences and channels

- The defined universes of audience potential (in other words, how many types of audience are within the same channel—for example, an office manager as well as a healthcare professional at a dermatologists office

- The reach (our targeted accounts as a percentage of the total market)

- The frequency (how many times you want to engage with the channel in a year)

- The number of calls per year

- The number of products supported and the weighting of each product by audience and channel

- Work days per year planned

- Percentage sales time vs. percentage travel time

- Hours worked per day

- Miles driven per day

- Cost of representative, including "extras" such as a car and laptop

- Cost per call, by type of call

- Extra sales gained from targeting an account

- New customers gained per year

- Multi-channel sales force – reps, call center, online, etc.

Working from this data, analytics can provide the best sales model for each channel, and learn whether a direct sales force (company sales reps, website, owned retail stores, etc.), an indirect sales force (wholesalers, distributors, dealers, internet intermediaries, etc.) or, most frequently, a mix of the two will prove to be the most successful.

Direct and indirect sales forces each have their own advantages. With direct sales forces, you have:

- Better control of selling activity

- Ownership of salesperson quality

- The ability to coordinate sales with other company functions

- A closer relationship with customers

With indirect sales forces, you have:

- Capabilities that are hard to replicate

- The ability to gain quick entry into a market

- Potential product synergy with indirect partner

- Possible efficiency gains

As with pricing and customer analytics, once sales metrics and channel data are in place, real-time models can be run to create the perfect balance of sales methods appropriate for the needed channels. Once again, an informed bet always trumps an easily-misplaced hunch.

OUR BRAND BELIEFS

When it comes to brands, all of us at Prophet work off the same basic understandings of how they work—and sometimes *don't* work. These beliefs come from our experience, as well as our extensive data collection and analysis. I'd like to end this chapter by sharing these "Brand Beliefs:"

- ### BRAND "ENTROPY" IS ALL TOO REAL

Without adequate marketing support (and the *right kind* of marketing support), the substance of a brand decays over time. Coca-Cola never takes their brand for granted and neither should you. That means paying as much attention to the brand's "big picture" as well as on-the-ground retail sales.

- ### BRANDS EXIST IN ECOSYSTEMS

Brands don't live in a vacuum; they're out in the marketplace, embedded in a specific internal context (product relationships and hierarchies) as well as a specific external context (partnerships and the product categories in which the brand is sold). You can't just artificially market a brand on its own, isolated from its surroundings. You have to look at systems of interacting brands.

- ### BRANDS ARE IMPORTANT ASSETS

Brands aren't just a vehicle to hit sales targets—they have a value all their own and should be regarded as a vital asset. Brand value should always be an important part of Market Analytics.

- ### MARKETING SHOULD BE VIEWED AS A MULTI-YEAR investment

Measuring the immediate impact of marketing only shows part of the picture—the real impact makes itself known over time. That's why long-term planning over the lifecycle of the product is vital, instead of just focusing on current campaign results.

- ## MARKETING SYSTEMS SHOULD BE INDUSTRY-SPECIFIC

Instead of applying the same marketing modeling to all business categories, specific multi-dimensional models that apply to the industry in question must be developed. Every business has its peculiarities that need to be addressed.

- ## DIGITAL MARKETING IS A MAJOR GAME-CHANGER

The digital revolution has significantly changed the marketing landscape in terms of reach, media usage and message control. That's why the proper mix of digital and non-digital marketing activities must be pursued in the 21st Century.

Marketing Analytics provides real-world solutions to marketing questions that formerly perplexed experts. When you put hard numbers and the right data visualizations to work, you uncover marketing methods unrivaled in their power and effectiveness. It may look like a Marketing Miracle—but in reality, it's grounded by a thriving and proven science.

ABOUT JAMES

James Walker

Senior Partner, Prophet

James Walker is a senior partner at Prophet. James, who has spent the last 20 years honing his skills and understanding of research and analytics across the spectrum of brand and marketing disciplines, leads Prophet's analytics practice. He splits his time between London and New York.

His diverse background embraces the analytical, the creative and the entrepreneurial. James founded Brand Science, which he and his partners later sold to Omnicom. He was a partner at Edge, which he sold to Accenture to create the kernel of Accenture Marketing Sciences. James was President International at AMS, and was an Accenture partner for 7 years.

Along the way, James was part of the launch team of the media agency MindShare, was one of J. Walter Thompson's youngest directors, owned the seminal The Clinic nightclub in London's Soho, and has made a number of feature films (including Fulham Noir and The Flower Girl) and worked on artistic projects with the UN amongst and other organizations. James is a frequent conference speaker, with contributions to TEDu and TEDx, and was a TEDGlobal host in 2011. James also speaks at many Marketing conferences ever year, is widely published, and also teaches at London Business School, Stern School Of Business at New York University, and INSEAD.

James' expertise in analytics includes brand research and analytics, brand equity modeling, marketing mix modeling, segmentation, econometrics, sales and marketing process improvement, among others. He has led consulting assignments in more than 40 countries, and has worked in most industries.

More recently prior to Prophet, James has helped launch and revitalize a variety of entrepreneurial ventures focused on both analytics and media. These included MOFILM, the World's largest crowd-sourcing creative agency where James is an investor and director; SSA & Company, a consultancy focusing on Six Sigma process improvement where James was a director and helped create a more 21st Century definition of Six Sigma and worked in partnership with a number of private equity houses; and Nunwood Consulting, a research firm, which James helped morph into the consulting space, spearheaded aggressive international expansion and helped pick up a number of awards.

James is a graduate of the London School of Economics and Political Science, the University of London.

CHAPTER 21

THE $20 MILLION DOLLAR MARKETING MIRACLE FORMULA

BY DC GILMAN

A s the summer sun beat down on me, the air was thick and the sweat dripped off my forehead in a steady stream. The sound of the roaring engine filled the Missouri air as I diligently mowed the lawns of twenty people on that sweltering Saturday afternoon. By all accounts, I had a thriving business…at the ripe age of eleven.

All I knew is that I did a good job—I was always on time and nice to all my customers. I even helped Mrs. Tilley get her groceries each week (without charging her). I probably could have, but she always tipped me more than I thought it was worth.

All the people talked to one another in that small town, and that talk was good for my business. The phone rang nearly every week with someone else who wanted me to mow their lawn. I had so much business that I enlisted my friends to help. I hired one to mow the lawns, one to follow behind for clean up, and another to handle the details and collect the money. I built it to a point where I had five friends working for me and when Saturdays rolled around, I could be found at the movie theater, playing or at the soda fountain.

My dad had taught me a lesson early on in life that proved invaluable as I grew up. The lesson was providing exceptional service and delegating as much as you can. I could have continued to mow the lawns and work both Saturday and Sunday and keep one hundred percent of the money. But I decided I didn't want to work both days of my weekend.

Another valuable lesson in that decision: I learned the real value of my time and taking time for myself.

My first corporate job was for one of America's largest printing companies. We focused primarily on printing magazines. As a family-owned company, the founders had instilled a strong culture that was centered around the customer and providing exceptional service consistently.

I started as an estimator and before I knew it, I was in sales. I continued to climb the ladder as the Vice President of Sales, and then moved into the role of Vice President of Operations shortly thereafter. In this role, I was technically second in command. I was directly under the President and the company was generating just under $15 million per year in revenue.

By many standards, it was a tremendously successful company. For me, I knew there was more out there; more customers, more revenue, more profit and more efficiency. When one of the owners wanted to retire, the brothers promoted me to President and I finally got my chance to demonstrate what I could do.

Deep down, I think, the brothers thought there would be a minimal transition when I took over; they assumed I would continue to run a smooth operation, with revenues remaining steady. Well, they underestimated me, that's for sure. As I took over, I came in like a bull in a china shop. At least that's the rumblings I heard years later.

For me, I was only doing what I had been eager to do for years. As I grew through the ranks, I knew all of the pitfalls, gaps, weaknesses and areas of inefficiency that were in the business. So, I started addressing them. I began with the operational issues internally. We saw an increase in operational efficiencies, streamlined work flow, reduced production schedules by fifty percent and actually increased on-time delivery by nearly twenty percent. I also implemented lean manufacturing skills which drove additional profit to the bottom line.

But the greatest miracle to happen in that two-year period? Pure marketing magic. When I was in the sales roles, I realized the company *talked* about caring for the customer—but talk and execution were two different things. It was about the ticket price, the sales volume and there was no taking into account the life-time value of a customer.

I had read enough books to know there was more revenue to be mined from our existing customers and more business in the market in general, but it would take a solid strategy to do it. I brainstormed and strategized, knowing the golden nuggets would be found in the little things.

I came back with the strategy to take the company to an entirely new level, and I knew it. I began to unveil piece by piece, knowing it would take some time to see the results. There were three categories that I focused on:

- Existing customers

- New customers

- Internal customers

With existing customers, I ran a list and broke them into three categories based upon revenues. Then I identified the additional incremental services we could provide that would generate more revenue than the cost of the service provided. Remember, my goal was to drive more profit to the bottom line, so this was an important component to the plan.

When I looked at the mid-tier revenue based customers, they were either near the lower end and almost in the bottom revenue category or at the top and almost in the higher revenue category. It was interesting and I found myself wondering what it would take to push the ones near the top over the edge and into the next revenue category, and nudge the ones at the bottom into the middle and upper revenue category.

I started calling the customers. Asking what they liked, what they didn't and what they thought was missing in our service offering. I uncovered the answers to take each customer to another level. It was interesting to me that none of our customers were working with us because of the price, which was good because we were not always the least expensive in the market…that's for sure.

For the smaller revenue category of clients, I analyzed the services they were purchasing from us. I uncovered a pattern and this pattern was worth a lot of money. Not in the actual services they were purchasing but rather in the services they *weren't*. The answer took me thinking in the opposite direction from what I would have normally thought.

It was revelation for me. Similar to looking at a painting where you see one figure instantly, yet the real figure is hidden in the opposite coloration of the image. That's what I finally saw. In all the years in sales and operations, the answer was there yet I had never seen it.

With one additional package offering, I discovered that we were missing an additional twenty percent of revenue. It was astonishing that there was that much additional revenue sitting on the table, just waiting for us to pick it up.

New customers aren't always as obvious as one would think either. Many think it is simply a function of reaching more prospects and increasing the conversion rates. I decided that would be too easy, so I approached the situation with the same mindset as I did with our smallest customers. Look for what is obvious and do the opposite.

What I found was that we were actually *turning away* business. Yes, turning it away. When I dug into it further, what I found was astonishing. The sales team was turning down jobs because the production in the plant would not handle the volume. If we couldn't get press time, then the jobs couldn't get printed.

The sales people had a "take it or leave it" attitude because it had been a problem for quite some time and no one knew about it. They chalked it up and just knew some jobs they could take and some they couldn't. A win some, lose some attitude.

I knew we had addressed the primary issues through the increased efficiencies we were seeing with the internal changes I had made. So I assured the sales team that we could take each and every job they brought into the system. If there was a job to be done, we could do it. Guaranteed.

This brings me to the last area I addressed: internal customers. What is an internal customer? It is the internal team, from your employees to the vendors your business works with. Often we overlook the fact that these people are actually customers as well. Customers in the sense that vendors have the ability to refer new clients, and employees from the sense that they have the ability to convert sales, refer sales and influence sales.

When I began this process, I didn't realize the issues we had with our internal customers was actually worse than what we had with our external customers. We had an internal morale issue and our vendors were being treated just as a "vendor." In my eyes, they were partners and some of our best customers. Yet in the eyes of our employees, they were merely someone expected to provide a good or service to the company.

How does one shift this attitude and mindset in a team of over 160? Well, I can tell you that it doesn't happen overnight and it also doesn't happen through a pep rally. It took strategy and thought to create the plan of attack for this issue.

I started with the employees first. I adopted a marketing campaign that was fun, challenging, and thought provoking—and just as importantly, revolved around making them proud, feel great and understand they were valued. My message of "value your employees as you would your best customers" quickly rippled throughout the company. The rumblings were positive and the air in the offices felt lifted. It was lighter, more fun and there was a sense of positive energy that resonated throughout the offices, which had never existed before.

Once the attitude shift with the internal employee had taken place, it was time to filter that out to the vendors. I changed all of the internal communication to read Valued Support Provider. I wanted the team to know, understand and appreciate that without our vendor's support, we would not have any business.

That was the last component I needed to implement. The process was complete, the wheels were in motion and I needed to sit back and be patient. Like the captain of the ship, you stay the course…and that's exactly what I did.

As I sat in my chair after two years in the President's seat, I watched the CFO bring in the report. It was the ultimate report card. I knew that we had been seeing significant increases, actual jumps in the numbers, but I didn't know the ultimate impact. As I reviewed the report, I leaned back, folded my arms behind my head and just smiled. I had done it. I had pulled it off. I had defied what the owners thought was possible and had taken the company from $15 million per year in revenue to *$21 million*. And, I did it in less than two years.

I grinned because I knew I had pulled off a marketing miracle. It wasn't one magic bullet. One statement. One approach. One client. One strategy. It was the ultimate success cocktail concoction that had proven potent, powerful and profitable. Then, I began to wonder how many other business owners out there were in the same situation and needed a marketing miracle.

After nearly another six months, I realized my heart and my passion was in helping entrepreneurs (especially young entrepreneurs). So I quit my job. Yes, I left a hefty six-figure salary and decided to become an entrepreneur.

As I reflected back on things, it was interesting I had been climbing the ladder all of my life. From starting out mowing lawns to working in the potato chip factory to radio shack to pumping gas to the printing company. I had actually ran out of ladder. I had reached the top rung and the only thing left for me was to jump to another ladder—but I would still be assuming the top rung on it, of course.

The lessons I learned in my career have certainly served me well and also provided a tremendous platform for me to help other entrepreneurs. In fact, I now share my marketing miracle formula and am excited to receive feedback from the businesses it has positively impacted.

Let me recap the $20 million dollar formula for you.

1. Existing customers – look at all aspects of your existing customers and apply this 3-pronged approach to increase revenues:

    a. Incremental Sales – what are the incremental sales that you may be overlooking? I challenge you to look at your existing customers and determine what areas and opportunities may be right in front of you yet are going unnoticed. Call your customers. It sounds so simple, yet it can be profound. The feedback and insight you gain lends to new ideas, new service offerings and many times discontinuation of service offerings.

 b. Play the Revenue Pick-Up Game – identify the new areas of service that you can be offering that have a nominal impact on your expense line yet yield a positive impact on the bottom line.

2. New customers – analyze the "Why" behind your sales process.

 a. Why aren't they buying?

 b. Why aren't they buying more?

 c. Why aren't they coming back more often?

  When you answer these three basic questions, the answers for your growth will be revealed.

3.. Internal customers – your employees and vendors are some of your best customers. Apply the 3-in-1 approach:

 a. Name three new programs that you can institute that will generate one new customer.

  Why limit it to one customer? You are not. If the approach will work to generate one, it will generate many.

You never realize the lessons you learn as a young entrepreneur and how they can impact you as an adult. In reflection, the marketing miracle formula I just shared with you stemmed from my first job mowing lawns when I was a child.

Get set, get ready and sit back enjoy the results. The ride is a journey, the experience is a blessing and the results are a joy.

ABOUT DC

DC Gilman worked his way up the corporate ladder from estimator through the sales ranks to Vice President of sales and ultimately President of a nationally recognized $21 million printing company. Under his leadership, sales outpaced production and he strategized and implemented operational efficiency systems, streamlined workflow, reduced production schedules by 50 percent and increased on-time delivery by nearly 20 percent. Through his laser-focused efforts, make-ready waste was reduced by 60 percent and annual revenues increased from $15 million to over $21 million under his leadership. He implemented lean manufacturing while managing over 160 employees nationwide.

DC left his successful position in 2011 to follow his passion and personal dream of building his own organization that fosters entrepreneurship. Knowing the positive impact that entrepreneurs have on the global economy, DC has dedicated his time, energy and efforts to providing proven tools, systems and knowledge. Through his various speaking engagements and efforts, he has taken what he learned growing up in a small town in Missouri—where he started his first business before he could drive and absorbed the strong work ethic that was instilled by his father—and combined this with the realistic approach of how to work smarter, not harder. This has formed the foundation and back bone for his educational platform.

Today, DC owns five companies and manages several streams of revenue—from network marketing to real estate—all by following the same advice and principles he shares with others. His no-nonsense approach shows entrepreneurs how to cut through the garbage, take action today, leverage cash flow and maximize opportunities and talents. For more information, go to www.DCGilman.com.

DC's latest book, *Get Your Win On!* showcases the essential steps, attitude and mindset for entrepreneurial success. DC was also selected as a contributing author for *Entrepreneurial Success Stories: How Common People Achieve Uncommon Results* with John Robinson and Loral Langemeier, scheduled for release late 2012. DC has been interviewed on various radio programs and has been featured in *USA Today* as a Game Changer.

DC has worked with and/or shared the stage with some of the top speakers, authors and renowned experts from around the world. He holds a Bachelor's degree in Business Administration from Central Missouri State University and is a graduate of the Dale Carnegie Course. DC and his wife Kathy have two teenage daughters, Mikaela and Alana, who they are assisting in building their own entrepreneurial empires. DC enjoys traveling, creative masterminds and learning about innovative business strategies.

CHAPTER 22

CREATING ONLINE MARKETING MIRACLES:

3 FOOLPROOF MAGNETIC MARKETING METHODS

BY DARRIN MISH

I f you're a fan of Dan Kennedy's marketing style (and I would think you would be if you're reading this book), you know he likes to be as outrageous as possible to get his message across.

Underneath that outrageousness, though, are tried-and-true marketing principles that always get the job done—the outrageousness is just the icing on the cake. That's why I love Dan—"crazy as a fox" is the perfect description of him. Even when his stuff seems the most unhinged, it's always carefully planned to make the right impact.

I may be a lawyer, but, in many ways, I'm a marketer at heart. A lot of people don't think Dan's techniques are right for an attorney such as myself, but as Dan says, they're made to work for *any* business. The alternative? Well, frankly, there really is no advantage to using the traditional (and expensive) methods of marketing, such as radio, TV and print, anymore. The fact is that audiences have been fragmented to such an extent that old media channels just don't work like they used to.

And that's okay. More than okay. Because I've become one of the top earners in my business by leveraging all the new (and, best of all, FREE!) online selling opportunities available. I've put them to work in innovative and exciting ways that leave my competition in the dust.

These days, the only offline marketing I really do is direct mail—which now actually works better than ever, because hardly anybody sends mail any more. That means *your* envelope has a much better chance of standing out (and here's a big secret to Direct Mail success: try to make sure your piece arrives on a Tuesday. Your message will almost always be sitting there all alone in the mailbox and attention WILL be paid!).

In this chapter, I'm going to tell you a few of my online marketing secrets— secrets that can work for any entrepreneur, professional or company—if you're willing to commit. These methods transform ordinary businesses into extraordinary money machines if you put these secrets to work.

THE BIG SECRET

Let's start by talking about Dan's concept of Magnetic Marketing. The way Magnetic Marketing works is your marketing does the work of attracting clients to *you*—you don't go chasing after them. Your job is to send a powerful message out into the marketplace, which causes interested people to "raise their hands." When they do, they're basically saying to you, "Tell me more," so you can confidently move on to the next step: converting that interest into a sale.

That's all well and good, but how do you build the all-important "magnetic" element into your marketing? How do you get people to *want* to listen to your message? How do you magnetize your marketing to attract the right leads?

Well, again, let's go back to the Book of Dan (or, actually, *books*, since he's written a whole bunch). Dan says prevention is almost impossible to sell, but offering "pain relief" can be a goldmine.

What does that mean, practically speaking? Well, let's say a parent wants their kids to wash their hands before eating. If the parent just says, "Wash your hands so you don't spread germs on your food and get sick," well, no kid is going to listen to that message. No Magnetic Marketing there!

However, if that same parent has kids who are way hungry and desperate for dinner, and that parent says, "I'm not serving dinner *until you wash your hands*"... well, all those little ones want is to make the pain of their rumbling stomachs to go away. The parent just told them that the only way to *make that pain go away* is if they wash their hands. *That* is a very magnetic message.

In my business, I've seen this principle work time and time again—and sometimes even against me. As a tax lawyer, I usually target people who already have big time pain from the IRS—I offer the relief they need. This works like crazy, because they need professional help to get through their tax problems.

So I thought about what would be the natural next step to create more revenue for my practice, and I had what I thought was a brilliant idea along those lines. What if I offered tax planning to people who had just survived their IRS escapades, so that I could make sure they never got in that kind of jam again?

Well, I went out and sold it with the systems that always worked so well for me...only this time, they didn't work so well. I think I had one sign-up in total. It turned out nobody was interested in stopping trouble from coming down the line—they only wanted to deal with it when it had already hit!

Remember, they don't sell pills to stop headaches *before* they happen; they sell them to make the ones you already have go away. That's why Magnetic Marketing focuses on pain and not prevention. Prevention isn't going to push someone into buying—but getting rid of some real pain is always an urgent matter.

MAGNETIC MARKETING METHOD #1: SEO

The internet is ideal for Magnetic Marketing because you have the ability to drive traffic to your website as well as deliver your message through a myriad of ways.

But how do you drive people to your website? How do you uncover the ones with the specific pain that you have the "prescription" for?

Well, the foundation of that process is to use SEO (Search Engine Optimization) tools to make the people who need your specific services come to *you* for that help—instead of your competition.

That starts with using the right keywords. When you dig in and do the right keyword research for your particular business, you can almost guarantee that you'll be attracting the exact right leads for your product or service.

Again, that means zeroing in on the "pain" from which your would-be customers are seeking relief. For my tax practice, I rely on keywords like "IRS Levy Relief" or "IRS Tax Help." When people search on these keywords on Google or any other search engine, my websites will rank high in the results. This process has helped me go from being mainly a local business to one with clients all across the country.

So...what problem do you solve? Why do people come to you for help?

Start by asking those questions and then, start making lists of sample keywords that people might search for, looking for answers. For example, if you're a chiropractor, a big keyword would probably be "back pain." If you're a dentist, you might look at "painless dentistry." Test out your keyword list with the free keyword tool that Google provides to see which ones motivate the most searches. Then, set up specific landing pages that are linked to those keywords and which sell the product or service that meets the leads' needs.

Most importantly, start "building your herd," as Dan Kennedy would say. That means include an offer of free information at your website, contingent on the visitor leaving his or her name and email address. This way, you can begin to build a marketing list that allows you to sell to these people down the line. They've already "raised their hands" and demonstrated interest in what you're selling—and those kinds of "warm leads" are obviously the best kind of leads to have.

Another great FREE SEO opportunity is Google Maps. This involves almost NO work on your part. You don't need to set up any websites or landing pages, you just have to fill in your info, upload any photos or videos you might want, and put it to work. All you have to do is log into Google maps with your Gmail account, list yourself as a local provider and then start entering the requested information.

Why is Google Maps so effective and important to your business? Well, when people use Google Maps to find a business, that means they're at an advanced stage of the buying process. As a matter of fact, they're probably in need of someone at that moment and looking at what their choices are. If your business ranks high on Google Maps, you'll have the opportunity to reach them at the precise moment every marketer waits for—the moment when they're ready to open their wallet and pay for your product or service.

Getting yourself at the top of that Google Maps search results page gives you a huge advantage in maximizing the opportunity in that moment. Generally speaking, if you get yourself at the top of the results, you'll get four times as many click-throughs as the next company down on the list. That's a massive amount of traffic you can have coming your way just by taking the proper steps. If you have some faithful customers who are willing to help you out by leaving some positive reviews of your business, that's going to really help your ranking along.

MAGNETIC MARKETING METHOD #2: VIDEO

Here are some statistics that should make you sit up and take notice. Online video viewers are expected to reach about 170 million this year. Over half of the population and over 70% of internet users will watch online video. Mobile video viewers will hit 55 million and Smartphone video viewers will hit 51 million.

That's a lot of potential customers for your business.

But video isn't just great marketing because of the numbers involved. It's also great marketing because people *get to know who you are* on their own terms, without having to actually come in to your office. There's no "social pressure" in watching a video—they can come to their own conclusions and decide whether they want to do business with you or not.

The fact is *people buy people* - and there's no better (or, let's face it, cheaper) way to put your personality out there than online video.

Now, let's talk a little bit about personality—because it's critical that you come across as authentic on camera. That means you shouldn't pretend you're something you're not, because people will smell a phony.

On the other hand, you should also not be afraid to be who you are; the more human you are, the more people will like you and be attracted to buy from you.

Case in point: I made one of my most memorable videos a few years ago and, to this day, people still ask me about it. Why? Because of a stupid accident that happened in the middle of recording it.

I was halfway through a video explaining an IRS tax matter when I accidentally knocked the microphone I had on the desk in front of me onto the floor. Well, of course, most people would have stopped recording and started over. I pride myself on *not* being "most people"—so I simply leaned over, picked up the mike and put it back on the desk and kept going—all while the camera was still rolling.

And *that's* what stuck in people's mind, more than anything else that came out of my mouth!

While you won't find many lawyers allowing themselves to be seen like that, I just thought it was a funny, human moment. I was already demonstrating my expertise in the content I was providing in the video, so I wasn't worried about not seeming professional. That's not usually a lawyer's problem. To be honest, most people are intimidated by lawyers, and I really believe that letting this "blooper" stand was a way to make them feel more comfortable about doing business with me.

Now, you might be reluctant to do your own videos. You might say, "I've got a face that's only good for radio." Well, I'm not exactly Tom Cruise either, but it doesn't matter. You just have to show that you know what you're talking about, you have solid solutions for your potential clients' problems and that you're personable and approachable. Just make sure you communicate clearly and concisely and avoid too much jargon or too many big words. Everyone needs to be able to understand your message.

Online video helps your SEO. Google gives it more weight than ordinary written content. It also allows you to be seen as a "celebrity," just as your local news anchorman would be, simply because you're on a form of

TV; people actually stop and stare when I walk through the lobby of my practice, because they recognize me from my videos.

So it's a complete win-win to build your own YouTube channel and also to imbed those videos on your website and on your social media pages... which brings us to our final Magnetic Marketing secret...

MAGNETIC MARKETING METHOD #3: SOCIAL MEDIA

Social media is where a lot of what I've been talking about comes together. The population of Facebook would make it the third biggest country in the world (behind China and India)—so, again, the numbers are certainly there!

Just like the videos, social media allows you to display your personality and be yourself. You will attract people who want to work with you based on that. I've posted some slightly controversial things on my Facebook page—I am a gun owner and I don't shy away from talking about it—but the truth is you shouldn't do business with someone who's going to judge you by things like that which don't really matter professionally.

You need to post regularly and you need to post articles, videos and blogs that again demonstrate that you're a trusted authority in your field (along with the personal stuff). Again, don't be afraid to have a little fun with your professional image. If you check out my Facebook page, you'll probably do a little bit of a double take at my profile photo—it was obviously taken at a professional photo session, but the face I'm making isn't exactly business-like!

But, again, that's okay—at least for my brand. The point is that the picture still looks like it's from a professional photo shoot - my expression just puts a little spin on the ball!

Personality-driven Magnetic Marketing attracts clients to any business, whether you or a lawyer, doctor, plumber or hardware store owner. It becomes an ongoing "Marketing Miracle" that builds your business without you having to do all that much work! So, if you're not already, put these three Magnetic Marketing methods to work for your enterprise. And please, feel free to visit my website at www.LawyersSecret.com for more information about how to create your own marketing miracles!

ABOUT DARRIN

Darrin Mish, Esq. graduated from Golden Gate University, in San Francisco, California, in 1993 with a Doctor of Jurisprudence. He was admitted to the Florida Bar in that same year and the Bar of the State of Colorado in 2002. He has earned an AV rating from Martindale-Hubbell, the country's most popular attorney rating service. An AV rating signifies an attorney that has "achieved the highest levels of professional skill and integrity." The AV rating is based upon peer reviews by other members of the Bar and the judiciary. Lawyers and judges in the larger community have been polled by Martindale-Hubbell and, based upon their submissions, the company has granted him the highest available rating for his legal skills, as well as for honesty and integrity. He has been honored to have his name placed in Martindale- Hubbell's Bar Register of Preeminent Lawyers as well.

This means that you, the client, receive aggressive representation from a young, energetic, honest, yet experienced attorney. Mr. Mish is permitted to practice before the United States Supreme Court; all courts of the State of Florida; the State of Colorado; the United States District Court, Middle District of Florida; United States Court of Appeals, 11th Circuit; United States Tax Court; United States Court of Federal Claims; the United States Court of Appeals, Federal Circuit; United States Court of Appeals, District of Columbia Circuit; and the United States District Court, Northern District of Florida. He has taken the extra steps to be admitted before all of these courts because he is committed to helping you with your IRS problems, including appeals.

In 2002, Mr. Mish was awarded "Practitioner of the Year" by the American Society of IRS Problem Solvers. He is a member of the Tax Freedom Institute, the American Bar Association, the National Association of Tax Professionals, the National Association of Criminal Defense Lawyers, the Florida Association of Criminal Defense Lawyers, and the Hillsborough County Bar Association. These memberships help him stay current with the law and enable him to protect your rights.

CHAPTER 23

FIVE MIRACLES TO HELP YOU TRANSFORM AND CONTINUOUSLY IMPROVE YOUR MARKETING AND YOUR BUSINESS

BY DALE GIBBONS

He said, "I'm gonna make you an offer you can't refuse."

Little did I know a series of "Miracles" was about to happen that would make me a new business owner and eventually help fulfill my dream of being financially free.

My friend Bob, who was also my boss at the time, had a struggling small business with a faint heartbeat across the hall from his newest entrepreneurial venture. He'd hired me a few months before to help him make his new business idea, unrelated to said struggling business, a success.

My only connection with the struggling business, which sold training for information technology professionals, was the water cooler. I know it sounds cliché, but it's where I'd go for a drink of water and the office scuttlebutt. Each time I went over for a sip, I felt I was standing in an emergency room, the patient fading fast and the ER staff pretending nothing was wrong. This business truly needed a miracle.

During my visits, I would chat with Peggy, the administrative assistant, as well as the other employees. Over the course of several weeks, I had put my finger on the pulse of the small company while everyone was too busy arranging deck chairs on the Titanic to even take notice of me.

Confident I had the cure, and sure I could help my friend wean it from his checkbook life support system, I'd make suggestions to him during our lunch meetings.

One day he said something that shocked me.

"Look" he said. "If you know so much about this business and how to fix it, then you need to own it."

I thought he'd lost his mind. First, I had very little cash to work with and had absolutely no idea how I was going to purchase a business. Second, why should I? I mean really, the business was losing money! In hindsight, maybe he should have given it to me! After all, not one of the sharks on ABC's Shark Tank would have invested. In fact, if it even made the show, it would be one of the crazy, goofball deals the producers slip in just for entertainment value.

"I'm not interested," I said. "I don't want to make your problem my problem."

I was confident the conversation was over, when he responded, "But Dale, you're missing the opportunity here. My problem is your opportunity because you have knowledge and experience I don't have. You can fix this business. I can't, and I just want to get my investment back."

Here's the rest of the story, and the miracles I've experienced that you too, can make happen in your own business:

MIRACLE #1: LEARNING TO HEAR AND DISCOVER WHAT PEOPLE *REALLY* BUY

On January 10, 2005, we signed the paperwork and I was the proud owner of a small business with a million dollars in annual sales.

I had learned throughout my career—and confirmed during my many meetings with my friend—that people really buy three things:

1. **Solutions** to their problems
2. **Experiences** that make them feel good
3. **Certainty**, security and peace of mind

Yes, we're complicated creatures and it's hard to fit all our motives for buying into three categories. But it's helpful to simplify things by separating the critical few from the helpful many, and the three above are the critical few, in my humble but accurate opinion.

Bob knew I had the solution to his problem. I had explained it to him in detail. He had worked with me for quite some time, and it had been a good experience for him. The solution and his good experience with me up to that point gave him enough certainty that his decision to make me an offer I couldn't refuse was a good one.

If you're having trouble in marketing or sales, it could be because you aren't tuned into what these three things are for your market. Whether it's one person across the lunch table or a list of a hundred thousand people, you'll need to ask good questions to truly *hear what they are saying* to understand what these three things are. Write these three things down on a note card before you write your next sales letter, go on your next sales call or, dare I say, try to get your kids to clean up their room.

There's more required though, than just understanding what people buy. We need to understand what they're willing to use to pay for it. Most assume people pay for things with money. But that's not really true.

In business, there are two primary currencies we all use in our transactions.

1. Time
2. Money

231

If you can't get someone to pay with their time, they'll never pay with their money. If they don't invest time to consider your offer, they won't buy. The trick is to understand what people really buy, then make your marketing worth something. More on this in the next miracle.

MIRACLE #2: CLARITY

One day during a meeting with all my employees (we had gone from fourteen to seven) I asked them what they thought our customers were willing to pay for.

I got seven different answers.

An important concept in continuous improvement is to define things clearly. We call these "operational definitions".

The operational definition of an operational definition is: A clear, unambiguous, description expressed in objective, usually measurable terms.

Here's the first, and most important operational definition I gave the team. It's the long pole in the continuous improvement tent, and everything we did in our business from the day I walked in as the new owner had to support it. I explained to the team that we had to focus our time on doing things people were willing to pay for. Our actions had to create *value*. Anything else was highly suspect. Here's your next operational definition:

Value: Anything people will pay for with their time or money.

Remember, the *anything* in our operational definition of value above is primarily three things. (See Miracle #1 if you've forgotten them.)

We went on to write several operational definitions, the most important of which was the definition of what people buy. We also developed the habit of asking ourselves "Is our customer willing to pay for what I'm doing right now?"

If the answer is no or you're not sure, Miracle #3 below will remove all doubt.

MIRACLE #3: LEARNING TO SEE

A church secretary received a phone call one day and the man on the line said with a southern drawl, "I'd like ta speak ta the head hawg uh the trough."

"Excuse me." The stunned secretary said.

"Well ma'am, I'm a lookin' fer the leader uh the church. Ya know, the head hawg."

Trying to not offend yet engineer a graceful exit, the secretary said, "Oh, I see. Well sir that would be pastor Russell and, well, we would never refer to him as a hog. Plus, he's on the phone now and can't possibly speak with you. Perhaps…"

The man interrupted, "Well now that thar's a cryin' shame, cuz I'm a farmer and jist sold some livestock. Got a perdy penny fer it too, and was a thinkin' I'd like ta make a ten thousand dollar donation to yer church."

Stunned by the man's words, the secretary quickly gathered her wits. "Well, sir, uh, well… will miracles never cease. It seems the big pig just finished his call and can speak with you now." She quickly connected the farmer to the pastor.

Clearly, the secretary saw no value in the farmer's words, at least not in the beginning. In fact, she was insulted. She certainly wasn't going to invest her or the pastor's time in this man. The farmer, too, didn't realize he was adding no value to the secretary. But the offer of a donation was irresistible. It added value, and that value changed *everything*. The money could certainly be a solution to a struggling church's problems. (See Miracle #1.)

So if value is anything people will pay for with their time or money, then what about the rest? What about the things they *won't* pay for? Wouldn't we want to know them, see them and minimize them?

Here's your third operational definition:

Waste: Anything people will *not* pay for with their time of money. In other words, it is non-value added activity.

For every dollar we spend on goods and services, only about a nickel is truly value added. The rest is waste.

Some waste, or non value-added activity, is required. There's nothing we can do but live with it. Filling out government paperwork comes to mind, unless you're a CPA and you client is paying you to do this for them.

Dan Kennedy taught me long ago that marketing is really anything and everything we can do to attract customers to our businesses. To me, marketing is creating and communicating value. In other words, it's the art and science of offering, getting a response and delivering the three things in miracle #1.

In order to create more value, you'll need to free up time and money by seeing waste in all its forms, and systematically eradicate it. There are nine forms of waste I look for in my businesses. Here are all nine, plus a couple examples of each. To help you remember them, let me introduce you to Timm P Wood:

TRANSPORTATION

"…the excessive delivery or movement of information, supplies or materials..."

- Delivering unneeded documents
- Over-addressing email distribution lists
- Cross-departmental resource commitments
- Excessive filing of documents
- Hand carrying paper to another process

INVENTORY

"…any supply of excess information, supplies or materials needed to produce goods or services just in time..."

- Files awaiting signatures or approvals
- Work awaiting task completion by others
- Obsolete files
- Obsolete equipment
- Outdated marketing materials
- Purchasing excessive supplies
- Insufficient training of back-ups

MOTION

"…any excess movement of people or machine needed to produce goods or services just in time…"

- Searching for computer files
- Searching for documents in file cabinets
- Repeatedly reviewing manuals for information
- Hand carrying paper or parts to another process
- Cross-departmental resource commitments without proper communications
- Not making something a priority for someone to complete

MARKETING

"…any effort that does measurably acquire new customers, increase sales with existing customers or increase the average transaction value…"

- 'Get your name out there' marketing
- Ads directed toward the wrong market
- Ads that don't communicate value and solicit a response
- Anything that creates negative word of mouth
- Brand advertising with no differentiation of offer to the market
- No understanding of what the market will buy

PEOPLE SKILLS

"…any appropriate people skills that are unutilized and not adding value…"

- Doing non-value added work
- Improper task to skills match
- Not making highest and best use of time
- Uneven workload
- Poor delegation and follow-up
- Micro-managing

WAITING

"...idle time created when people wait for people, people wait for machines, and machines wait for people..."

- Excessive signatures or approvals
- Delays in receiving information
- Cross departmental resource commitments
- Dependency on others to complete tasks
- Computer software revision problems
- Not a priority for someone to complete

OVER-PROCESSING

"...any effort which adds no value to the product or service..."

- Producing reports no one reads or needs
- E-mailing, faxing the same document multiple times
- Ineffective meetings
- Making extra copies
- Entering repetitive information on multiple documents

OVERPRODUCTION

"...producing more or faster than needed to produce goods or services just in time..."

- Duplicating reports or information
- Too much information being shared
- Ineffective meetings and no agendas
- Repetitive data entry
- Constantly revising documents
- Poor project planning

DEFECTS

"…inspection, repair or rework of a product or service..."

- Data entry errors
- Forwarding incomplete documentation
- Incorrect information on document
- Not appropriate staffing to service customer

- Pricing errors
- Lost files or records
- Inefficient file system on desktop PC or in cabinet
- A/P and A/R errors
- Audit findings

MIRACLE #4: THE POWER OF HELPING OTHERS SEE, TOO

When I first met with the sales team, I was frustrated with the information they were giving me about their sales pipelines and what they were doing to move deals toward closing. We pored over excel spreadsheets and each sales rep would talk about the deals they were working on. They droned on about why it was a good deal and sure to close.

After about three weeks of the same old shell game, I'd had enough. There was a large 4 x 8 white board in the meeting room of our office, and I decided it was time to drain the swamp on our marketing and sales system to see what was really going on. It was time to implement *visual management* of our marketing and sales process.

I went to the office the next Saturday when I knew I'd have the place to myself. I cleaned the board and drew vertical black lines that made five columns. Each column had a label at the top. It looked something like this:

25	50	75	90	100

I then wrote operational definitions for each of these phases. There were very specific criteria that a deal had to meet in order to be placed into a phase.

The next Monday, the sales team filed into the meeting room as usual, excel sheets in hand.

They looked nervously at the board. I handed each sales rep their own colored super sticky PostIt™ note pad. I then handed them copies of the operational definitions of a lead, a prospect, a customer etc. Also included were the operational definitions and criteria for each phase of the pipeline.

"Take thirty minutes and use the template I've created for you to transfer your deals from your Excel spreadsheet to the pipeline board. You have your unique colored sticky note. Once you're sure your deal matches the criteria I've written for you, add it to the board in the correct phase."

I then left them to finish their assignment.

When I returned, I was amazed at what I saw. One of the reps, I'll call him Dennis, suddenly had just one deal that was worth talking about. Most of his "pipeline" evaporated because his deals did not meet the new criteria.

Eight years later, we've refined this substantially. And every morning, we have a 30-minute team huddle to discuss the board and what each rep is doing to move the deal toward close, what help they need, what marketing sequence each prospect is for each step, etc.

MIRACLE #5: A SMOOTH FLOWING STREAM

Over the years, we've refined the way we manage our marketing and sales process. The business has grown 8 fold and has been an Inc. 5000 honoree multiple times.

One of the transformational steps in our success has been to think of our sequence of value-adding activities as a "value stream". Here's how to picture it in your mind's eye for your business:

Someone raises their hand from the masses in response to your now *valuable* marketing message, and we help them into your boat.

They're now on a journey down the value stream with you. They can leave at any moment if you stop adding value. If you fail to solve their problem, create a good experience or make them feel certain their decision was a good one, they're gone. There are boats standing by to take them off (competitors, your own risk reversal and guarantees).

Invest a little time in mapping your value stream and learning to see and eliminate waste, and you could experience the same miracles I have over the last eight years.

Smooth sailing!

ABOUT DALE

Dale Gibbons is an entrepreneur, writer and speaker. He owns two businesses and publishes a monthly newsletter on business development topics. Dale is a graduate of Purdue University and he began his career in the aerospace industry in 1987, as a field service liaison with General Electric's aircraft engine group. After working 18 years with firms like GE, Compaq, EDS and Manpower, Inc., Dale acquired a small, struggling technology firm in 2005. While applying his passion for process improvement, marketing and sales, he reinvented the business, which is now ranked 4th on the Business First list of 50 largest Louisville, KY, area technology firms and has made the Inc. Magazine list of fastest growing private small businesses in the U.S.

After turning the tech firm around, Dale replaced himself in 2008 and currently plays a passive role of coach and advisor to the management team. Dale founded The Continuous Improvement Center in 2008, consulting with businesses on process improvement and performance excellence. He also serves as Vice President, COO with Farm Credit Mid-America, one of the nation's largest lenders to farmers and rural Americans.

Dale is active with the Kentucky Center for Performance Excellence, where he serves on the operating committee and also as a certified examiner for the Malcom Baldrige Performance Excellence Award. Dale also serves on the board of directors of Junior Achievement of Kentuckiana. He can be reached at www.TheCICenter.com.